JUV/
GV
903.5
.N33
2002

W9-CDO-166

R0401378010

Bowling for beginners : simple steps to

Bowling for Beginners

Simple Steps to Strikes & Spares

DISCARD

Oriole Park Branch
7454 W. Balmoral Ave.
Chicago, IL 60656

Bowling for Beginners

Simple Steps to Strikes & Spares

Don Nace

Photographs by Bruce Curtis

Sterling Publishing Co., Inc.
New York

Oriole Park Branch
7454 W. Balmoral Ave.
Chicago, IL 60656

DISCARD

To my wife, Terri, for all her patience during the writing of this book. To my daughter Melissa for her typing, and all her help with this book. To my son Anthony for proofreading, and my daughter Denise just for being Denise, and for all of the e-mail that went back and forth. To my grandson, Cole, for being good when his mother was doing the typing.

Acknowledgments

Thanks to AMF Worldwide, and Richie, the manager of AMF Wantagh Lanes, for the use of his bowling center in Wantagh, Long Island. To Dottie for arranging the time the lanes could be used. I would also like to thank the children in the scholarship league at Wantagh Lanes, and especially Frannie, Teri, Chris, and Logan. Thanks to Jim Hallahan for the use of 300 Bowl in Massapequa Park, New York. A special thanks to Chris for the use of his Pro Shop, Chris Keller Sport Stop Bowler's Shop in Bayshore, Long Island. I would also like to thank some of the great coaches I studied under: Fred Borden, Palmer Fallgren, Bill Hall, Ron Hoppe, Dick Ritger, Dr. Jeff Briggs, exercise specialist, and Dr. Eric Lasser, sports psychologist.

Edited by Isabel Stein

Library of Congress Cataloging-in-Publication Data

Nace, Don.
 Bowling for beginners : simple steps to strikes & spares / by Don Nace ; photographs by Bruce Curtis.
  p. cm.
 Includes index.
 ISBN 0-8069-4968-6
  1. Bowling—Juvenile literature. [1. Bowling.]
 I. Curtis, Bruce, ill. II. Title.

GV903.5 .N33 2001
794.6—dc21

00-048268

10 9 8 7 6 5 4 3 2 1

First paperback edition published in 2002 by
Sterling Publishing Company, Inc.
387 Park Avenue South, New York, N.Y. 10016
© 2001 by Don Nace
Distributed in Canada by Sterling Publishing
^{c}/o Canadian Manda Group, One Atlantic Avenue, Suite 105
Toronto, Ontario, Canada M6K 3E7
Distributed in Great Britain and Europe by Chris Lloyd
at Orca Book Services, Stanley House, Fleets Lane,
Poole BH15 3AJ, England.
Distributed in Australia by Capricorn Link (Australia)
Pty. Ltd., P.O. Box 704, Windsor, NSW 2756 Australia
Printed in China
All rights reserved

Sterling ISBN 0-8069-4868-6 Hardcover
    0-8069-7450-8 Paperback

Contents

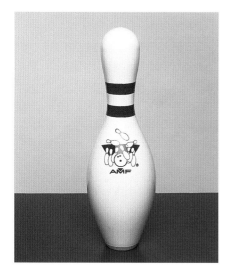

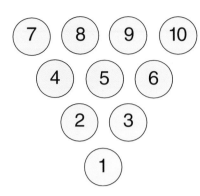

Introduction

As long as there have been humans, there probably has been bowling in some form. Over 6,000 years ago, in ancient Egypt, people bowled. We know this because tall, thin stones and balls have been found in graves there. An early form of bowling, boccie, was introduced in England by the Romans in the 12th century and it has been popular in some form ever since as lawn bowling.

There are more than 100,000,000 bowlers in 90 countries worldwide. Bowling is the #1 participatory sport in the United States and is very popular in the United Kingdom as well. In the 1998–99 Bowling League Season, there were over 68,000 registered League Bowlers in Canada.

One of the main reasons bowling is so popular is that bowling is fun. Whether you are young or old, big or

small, male or female, you can compete successfully. It takes practice, a positive mental attitude, and dedication.

If you want to, you can join a bowling club or league. There are many different leagues, including adult, child, female, male, mixed male and female, and senior leagues. There are leagues for small children, in which the channel (gutter) on the side of the lane is blocked so the ball can't roll off there. Handicap leagues try to equalize competition by giving the lower-scoring bowlers a score advantage to start with, making it possible for bowlers of different averages to compete against each other. In scratch leagues, only the pins you knock down count. You do not get any extra pin advantage, as you do in a handicap league.

This book will teach you the basics so you can join the fun world of bowling. If you are already bowling, it will give you pointers on how to improve your game.

Whether you are a student, a coach, or a great player, in bowling you never stop learning. Read everything you can, listen to it all, and watch everyone. Always keep an open mind when becoming exposed to and learning something new. Not every coach agrees on everything or every type of technique. People are different; therefore, we must do what is best for us and use our abilities to make our game better.

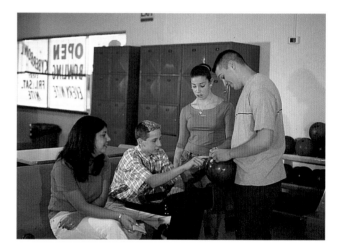

Chapter 1
The Basics

Like every game, bowling has its own special words. As we come to new words, we'll explain them, and you can find most of them in the glossary at the end of the book too. The lane or alley is the wooden playing surface. The pins are the tall, curved wooden targets you are aiming at. They are arranged in a triangle at the far end of the lane. Basically, bowling is a simple game. The goal is to roll the ball down the lane to knock down the pins.

There are standard measurements for lanes, bowling pins, and bowling balls, and standard rules of how to play. This way,

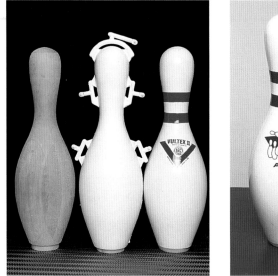

Pins being made.

Finished pin.

The numbers of the bowling pins.

people everywhere can compete under basically equal conditions.

The Pins

There are 10 pins in all, arranged in a triangle that is 36 inches (91.5 cm) on a side. Each pin has a position number, although the numbers aren't written on the pins. See the diagram for the numbers of the pins. The #1 pin is also called the head pin. Learn the numbers, as you will need them later on.

A pin is 15 inches (38 cm) tall, 3 inches (7.6 cm) wide, and weighs not less than 3 lbs. 6 oz. (1512 g), but not more than 3 lbs. 10 oz. (1624 g). The pins are made of maple wood or maple wood covered with plastic.

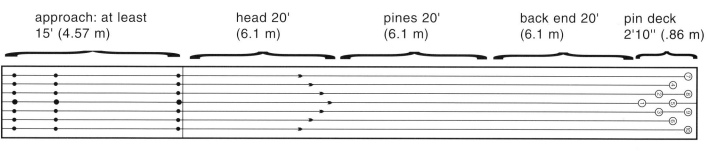

| approach: at least 15' (4.57 m) | head 20' (6.1 m) | pines 20' (6.1 m) | back end 20' (6.1 m) | pin deck 2'10" (.86 m) |

The parts of a lane.

The Approach and Bowling Lane

The Approach

The area you walk on to deliver (roll) your bowling ball is called the approach. It is the part before the start of the lane. The approach is made of maple wood, and usually is 16 feet (4.88 m) long. It must be at least 15 feet (4.57 m) long. The approach is where you will be taking your steps and releasing your bowling ball when you roll it onto the lane.

The Bowling Lane

Dividing the approach from the beginning of the lane is the foul line. A bowling lane has four parts. The first 20 feet (6.1 m) of the lane is called the head. It is made of maple wood, a very hard wood. The next 20 feet is called the pines, and is made of pine wood, which is softer. The third 20 feet is also made of pine and is called the back end (see diagram). The area on which the pins sit is called the pin deck.

The lane is 40 inches (101.6 cm) wide and is 39 boards wide. From the foul line to the end of the lane is 62 feet 10 inches (19.15 m). From the foul line to the head pin (the #1 pin) is 60 feet (18.3 m). There is a channel that runs along each side of the bowling lane, also called the gutter.

Targeting Aids

A set of dots and arrows, called the Rangefinder system, is marked on the approach and lane to help you aim. They will also help you to know where to stand when you start a shot. This system was developed by the Brunswick Bowling Ball Company during World War II. It is important to know where these dots and arrows are. They help make adjustments to your delivery easier.

Generally there are 3 sets of target dots on the approach (see above). The dots are placed on every fifth board, counting from the outside. (A right-handed bowler counts dots, boards, and arrows from the right; a left-handed bowler counts dots, boards, and arrows from the left.) The large central dot is always on the 20th board, for both right- and left-handers.

One set of dots is 2 inches (5 cm) before the foul line. One set is 12 feet (3.66 m) before the foul line. A third set is 15 feet (4.57 m) before the foul line. Sometimes the dot sets at 12 and 15 feet do not have all 7 dots, but only 5. Always check to see how many dots there are. About 6 feet (1.83 m) beyond the foul line is another set of small dots, located on boards 3, 5, 8, 11, and 14 from the outside.

There are 7 guiding (target) arrows marked on the lanes. Once you learn how to use them, they will help you to position yourself and aim consistently when you bowl, because the arrows are in a direct line with (on the same board with) the pins on the lane, but are much closer to you than the pins are. The closest arrows are about 15 feet (4.57 m) beyond the foul line. An arrow is marked on every fifth board across. The center arrow is on the same board as the center dot (20th board).

The #1 and #5 pins are in line with the center arrow. The #3 and #9 pins are in line with the third arrow from the right. The #6 pin is in line with the second arrow from the right. The #2 and #8 pins are in line with the third arrow from the left. The #4 pin is in line with the second arrow from the left. The #7 pin is in line with the leftmost arrow.

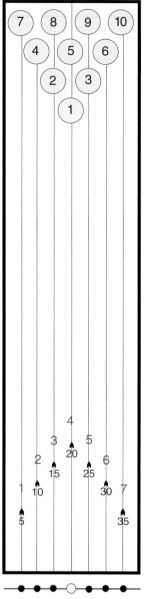

Lefty: Numbering of arrows (red type) and boards (black type).

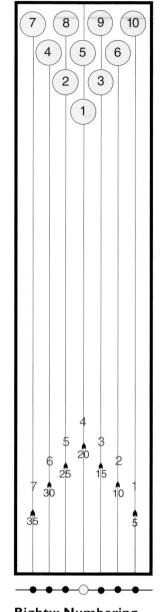

Righty: Numbering of arrows (red type) and boards (black type).

Scorekeeping

There are 10 frames to a game. You get two chances in a frame to knock down the pins. (Pins knocked down are automatically removed after each roll of the ball by a machine called a pinsetter.) Then it is your opponent's turn. When you knock down all 10 pins with your first ball, it is called a strike, and your turn ends. When you knock down some pins with your first ball in the frame and knock down the remainder of the pins on your second ball of the frame, it is called a spare.

Your scores are totaled on a scoresheet or scoreboard. Most bowling centers now have computerized scoring. All you have to do is follow the directions on the computer, and the computer will do the scoring for you. However, it's good to understand how the scores are calculated. Each of the big boxes on the scoresheet represents a frame. Each big box has a little box in the right-hand corner. The number of pins knocked down on the first ball of the frame is marked to the left of the little box. The number of pins knocked down on the second ball of the frame (if there is one) is marked inside the little box. In the large part of the box, the total score you have so far is added together to the previous total.

Strike. If all the pins are knocked down on the first delivery (roll of the ball) of the frame, mark an X in the little box; this symbol indicates a strike. That is the end of your turn for that frame. Next time it is your turn, the pinfall (number of pins you knock down) for the next two balls is added onto the total in the previous frame, as well as onto its own frame (in effect, it is added twice).

Miss or error. If you do not knock any pins down on the first ball of a frame, you put a dash (–) to the left of the small square for that frame. If you do not knock any pins down on the second ball of the frame either, put a dash in the little box. This is the symbol for a miss or error.

Spare. If you knock down some of the pins on the first ball of the frame and the rest with the second ball, mark the number of pins you knocked down on the first ball to the left of the little square, and mark a slash in the small square (/). This is the symbol for a spare. That is the end of your turn. In the frame in which you made a spare, you get 10 points for making the spare, and also add in the pinfall from the first ball you roll in the next frame when it is your turn again.

Tenth Frame. In the tenth frame, there are three little squares. You get at least 2, and possibly 3 shots in the 10th frame. The first pinfall you mark in the

A strike.

The 9–10 spare.

The 6–7 split.

first little square on the left, the second pinfall in the second little square. If there is third roll of the ball, you mark that in the last little square. If you get a strike on your first roll, you get to go twice more. If you get a spare on your second roll in the tenth frame, you get to go again. If you bowled a perfect game, getting a strike in the first 9 frames and 3 strikes in the tenth final frame, you would get a score of 300.

 Foul. The foul line is a dark dividing line separating the end of the approach from the beginning of the bowling lane. During league play, there is a beam of light that goes continuously across the foul line. The idea is to release the ball without having your foot or any other body part go over or touch the foul line. If you touch or go over the foul line, you have made a foul. If this happens during league play, a buzzer will sound and another light will identify on which lane the foul occurred. If you make a foul on the first ball of the frame, you reset all the pins and you get to throw one more ball. No pins that were knocked down on the first ball count, however. If it happens on the second ball of the frame, any pins knocked down with that ball do not count. (In that case, only count the pins knocked down by the first ball, if it was not a foul.)

 Split. A split occurs when pins are left standing that are not next to each other. On your scoresheet, you mark it with an S, or a circle around the number

Chris approaches the foul line.

Symbol for split spared.

of pins knocked down on the first ball of the frame. It is harder to make a spare when your first ball has created a split than it is without the split. If you do succeed in making the spare, it is called a split spared.

Here are some examples of scoresheets, with explanations of how scoring works.

Scoresheet Example 1

Game 1: What Happened

Frame 1: You get a strike.

Frame 2: You get a strike.

Frame 3: You get a strike.

Frame 4: You knock down 5 pins on your first ball. You knock down 3 pins with your second ball.

Frame 5: You knock down 7 pins with your first ball, and leave a split. You knock down all 3 of the pins of the split with your second ball (you "convert your spare").

Frame 6: You get a strike.

Frame 7: Your foot crosses the foul line on the first ball (score of 0). You knock down 9 pins with the second ball.

Frame 8: You knock down 8 pins with the first ball. You knock down the remaining 2 pins with the second ball.

Frame 9: You knock down 8 pins with your first ball. You knock down 0 pins with the second ball.

Frame 10: You make a strike with your first ball. You make a strike with your second ball. You knock down 8 pins with the third ball.

Game 1: How the Scoresheet Is Calculated

Frame 1:
10 points for strike in Frame 1 plus next 2 balls, which are:
10 for strike in Frame 2
10 for strike in Frame 3
Total Frame 1: 30

Frame 2:
10 for strike in Frame 2 plus next 2 balls, which are:
10 for strike in Frame 3
5 for first ball in Frame 4
30 total from Frame 1
Total Frame 2: 55

Frame 3:
10 for strike in Frame 3 plus next 2 balls, which are:
5 for first ball in Frame 4
3 for second ball in Frame 4
55 total from Frame 2
Total Frame 3: 73

Scoresheet for Game 1.

NAME	1	2	3	4	5	6	7	8	9	10
1	X 30	X 55	X 73	5 3 81	7 Ø 101	X 120	F 9 129	8 ╱ 147	8 – 155	X X 8 183
2										

Frame 4:   5 for first ball in Frame 4
              3 for 2nd ball in Frame 4
             73 total from Frame 3
             Total Frame 4: 81

Frame 5:   7 for first ball in Frame 5
              3 for second ball in Frame 5, plus next ball (because of spare), which is:
             10 from Frame 6
             81 total from Frame 4
             Total Frame 5: 101

Frame 6: 10 from strike plus next two balls, which are:
              0 for first ball in Frame 7
              9 for second ball in Frame 7
            101 total from Frame 5
             Total for Frame 6: 120

Frame 7:   0 for first ball in Frame 7
              9 for second ball in Frame 7
            120 total from Frame 6
             Total for Frame 7: 129

Frame 8:   8 for first ball in Frame 8
              2 for second ball in Frame 8, plus next ball, because of spare, which is:
              8 from Frame 9
            129 total from Frame 7
             Total for Frame 8: 147

Frame 9:   8 for first ball in Frame 9
              0 for second ball in Frame 9
            147 total from Frame 8
             Total for Frame 9: 155

Frame 10: 10 for first ball
              10 for second ball
               8 for third ball
             155 total from Frame 9
             Total for Frame 10: 183

Scoresheet Example 2

Game 2: What Happened

Frame 1: You knock down 5 pins with your first ball and 5 pins with your second ball.

Frame 2: You get a strike (knock down all 10 pins with the first ball).

Frame 3: You knock down 3 pins with your first ball and 7 pins with the second ball.

Frame 4: You get a strike.

Frame 5: You knock down 4 pins with the first ball and 6 pins with the second ball (make a spare).

Frame 6: You knock down 2 pins with the first ball and 3 pins with the second ball.

Frame 7: You get a strike.

Frame 8: You foul with the first ball and knock down 4 pins with the second ball.

Frame 9: You knock down 6 pins with the first ball and 4 pins with the second ball.

Frame 10: You get a strike with the first ball.

You knock down 7 pins with the second ball.

You knock down 2 pins with the third ball.

NAME	1	2	3	4	5	6	7	8	9	10
1	5 ◢ 20	X 40	3 ◢ 60	X 80	4 ◢ 92	2 3 97	X 111	F 4 115	6 ◢ 135	X 7 2 154
2										

Scoresheet for Game 2.

Game 2: How the Scoresheet Is Calculated

Frame 1:
- 5 points for first ball in Frame 1
- 5 points for second ball in Frame 1 plus the next ball, which is:
- 10 points for strike in Frame 2

Total Frame 1: 20

Frame 2:
- 10 points for strike in Frame 2, plus next two balls, which are:
- 3 points for first ball in Frame 3
- 7 points for second ball in Frame 3
- 20 points total from Frame 1

Total Frame 2: 40

Frame 3:
- 3 points for first ball in Frame 3
- 7 points for second ball in Frame 3, plus next ball (because of spare), which is:

- 10 points for strike in Frame 4
- 40 points total from Frame 2

Total Frame 3: 60

Frame 4:
- 10 points for strike in Frame 4, plus next two balls, which are:
- 4 points for first ball in Frame 5
- 6 points for second ball in Frame 5
- 60 points total from Frame 3

Total Frame 4: 80

Frame 5:
- 4 points for first ball in Frame 5
- 6 points for second ball in Frame 5, plus next ball (because of spare), which is:
- 2 points for first ball in Frame 6
- 80 points total from Frame 4

Total Frame 5: 92

Frame 6:
  2 points for first ball in Frame 6
  3 points for second ball in Frame 6
92 points total from Frame 5
Total Frame 6: 97

Frame 7:
10 points for strike in Frame 7, plus next two balls, which are:
  0 points for first ball in Frame 8
  4 points for second ball in Frame 8
97 points total from Frame 6
Total Frame 7: 111

Frame 8:
  0 points for first ball in Frame 8
  4 points for second ball in Frame 8
111 points total from Frame 7
Total Frame 8: 115

Frame 9:
  6 points for first ball in Frame 9
  4 points for second ball in Frame 9, plus next ball (because of spare), which is:
10 points from first ball in Frame 10
115 points total from Frame 8
Total Frame 9: 135

Frame 10:
10 points for first ball in Frame 10
  7 points for second ball in Frame 10
  2 points for third ball in Frame 10
135 total from Frame 9
Total Frame 10: 154

Chapter 2
Bowling Etiquette and Safety

Here are a few simple things to keep in mind, so that you and the people you play with will have an enjoyable and safe time at the bowling lanes.

Some Important Rules

1. Take care of the equipment. Try not to loft or toss the ball far out onto the lane, where it will damage the lane's surface.

2. Balls can be a danger to fingers. When picking up a ball off the ball return, do it carefully to avoid getting your fingers caught between two bowling balls. Grasp the ball

Pick up the ball at the sides so your fingers can't get bumped by returning balls.

from the sides, where the balls will not hit together.

3. Be sure the holes in the bowling ball fit your hand. (You can tighten them with tape inside the holes if they are too loose, as a temporary solution.) If too tight, your fingers may get jammed or sprained. If too loose, you could lose control of the ball and hit someone with it.

4. Be aware of what is going on around you. Before you step up onto the approach to bowl, check for clearance on both sides. Don't bowl if someone else is bowling in the lane next to you. Before you take any practice swings, look around you to be sure you have enough room.

5. Don't distract anyone else during their setup with noise or sudden movements.

6. Don't roll a second ball until the first one has returned.

7. Don't use anyone else's ball without permission.

8. Keep your personal items (bowling balls, equipment) out of the traffic areas where someone might trip on them.

9. If there is moisture on your bowling shoes, the soles will become sticky even if they are only slightly wet. That will cause the shoe to stick when you are in a slide to deliver the ball. This can be very dangerous. Don't put ashes, baby powder, or any other substances on the soles of your bowling shoes. They can cause someone to slip. If you think anything might be on them, wipe the soles right away. Keep food and beverages out of the bowling areas. On rainy or snowy days, do not leave the bowling area with your bowling shoes on. If your shoes become sticky, use sandpaper or a wire brush to clean the bottoms.

Tape can be added to a hole to make the fit a little tighter.

Some people wear a slipper when off the approach to protect the sole of the sliding foot.

Wipe your bowling ball with a towel after each use, to remove lane conditioning oil.

10. Never step beyond the foul line onto the lane. You might pick up lane conditioning oil and track it back onto the approach, which could cause someone to slip or stick on the approach.
11. Never roll a ball toward the pins if someone is working on the pinsetter.
12. Never bowl in street shoes.
13. Be courteous and positive to the people around you. Don't give advice unless someone has asked you.

Warmup Exercises

More acute injuries occur during the first dozen or so shots than at any other time in bowling. Many sports have a warmup routine that the athletes go through before they start the sport activity. In bowling, you should also warm up. Start with an aerobic activity for about 5 minutes. This could be walking on a treadmill, bike riding, jogging in place, doing jumping jacks, or some other light but vigorous activity that will increase your body temperature. Start slowly and build up intensity gradually. Then do stretching slowly. Stretch as far as you can in your range of motion, but stop when your muscles begin to hurt. Hold the stretch for 15 to 30 seconds; then slowly relax to your original position.

Stretch for front of thigh muscles (quadriceps).

Quadriceps. These are the muscles that make up the front of the thigh. Balance on one leg while grasping the foot of the other leg with the opposite arm behind your back. Pull the foot back towards the opposite buttock. Alternate with the other leg. This will stretch the muscles of the front of the thigh.

Calves. Space your feet 1 to 2 feet (30 to 61 cm) apart, with one foot in front. Supporting yourself on your front leg, slowly lean forward, stretching the calf muscle of the rear leg, keeping both feet flat on the ground. Hold this for 15 to 30 seconds. Repeat with the other leg, and continue, alternating legs.

Shoulder and Rotator Cuff. The rotator cuff muscles motor your shoulder joint. Move one arm across the front of the chest. With the opposite hand pressing on the triceps muscle behind the elbow joint, stretch the shoulder. Repeat with other arm and continue, alternating arms.

Stretch for calf muscles.

Stretch for shoulder and rotator cuff.

Wrist and Forearm. Extend one arm fully in front of the body with the palm facing out and hand bent upward at the wrist. Using the opposite hand, apply pressure to the fingers, pulling them toward your body. This will stretch the flexor muscles. Hold the stretch for 15 to 30 seconds. Once the stretch is completed, turn the hand downward at the wrist. Pull the fingers toward your body. This will stretch the forearm extensors. Repeat with the other arm and continue, alternating arms. The flexors are the muscles that bend your limbs or body parts; the extensors are the ones that extend them.

Stretches for wrist and forearm.

Balance

Balance is a very important part of bowling and of everyday life. When you are in the approach (the steps and swing during delivery), you have a heavy bowling ball swinging at your side from the front to the back of you. If you have been missing your shots, bad balance could be the reason.

A drill you could use to help improve your balance is to stand on one leg for 30 seconds, and then switch to the other leg. Do this for several minutes. Your goal is to do this with your eyes closed. Doing this with your eyes closed will really help your balance.

Chapter 3
Equipment

Here we'll talk about balls, gloves, and shoes, your basic equipment.

The Ball

Choosing a House Ball

If you have just started bowling, you are probably using a "house ball," one provided by the bowling center. Here are some things to look for in a house ball as far as fit goes:

■ Thumb hole: You should be able to move your thumb in and out with one side of thumb touching the hole and the other touching just barely.

The holdout test helps you know if a ball is the right weight for you.

- Be sure to get a ball that is drilled for conventional grip, with holes deep enough to insert your fingers in to the 2nd knuckle if you are a beginner.
- Weight: Choose the heaviest ball you can use comfortably. The ball should not be so heavy that you have to squeeze it to hold it on your hand. You should be able to swing it without having it pull your shoulder out of line. A general guideline is that the ball should be about one-tenth of your weight. Do a holdout test for weight: Extend your arm with the elbows locked. Hold the ball in your bowling hand, supported by your second hand underneath your bowling hand. If you can't hold the ball that way for at least 5 seconds, it is too heavy.

There are some problems about using a house ball, including the following:

- Holes in a house ball are drilled so they can be used for either hand, so the holes may be too big because the 3rd and 4th finger holes are drilled the same size.
- If thumb holes fit, the others are too loose.
- The ball may be too top-heavy, which could affect how it moves on the lane.

Your Own Bowling Ball

There are advantages to having your own bowling ball. You will be able to learn more consistently with equipment that doesn't vary, and it will be designed exactly for your hand and chosen to fit your needs. In addition to this chapter, see Chapter 6 for more detailed information about bowling balls.

The bowling ball is a major piece of equipment for the bowler, although not the only equipment needed. The dimen-

Young children can enjoy bowling also. They should use a lightweight bowling ball.

sions and materials allowed are standardized. A bowling ball can be up to 27 inches (68.6 cm) in circumference (8.595 inches or 21.8 cm in diameter), and the weight range can be from 6 to 16 lbs (2.6 to 7.2 kg). A young child would use a lightweight ball.

What Bowling Balls Are Made Of

Early in the history of bowling, balls were made of stone, then wood, and then rubber. Now they are plastic, urethane, or reactive resin. The finger and thumb holes of bowling balls today are commonly drilled over the label on the ball. Early bowling balls were made of three pieces: the core, a pancake type weight block, and the shell. In the early 1980s, a two-piece ball was developed. It is made up of a weight block of heavier material, which may be in one of many different shapes, and the outer shell.

The material of the ball — polyester plastic, urethane, or reactive resin — affects how it behaves. Another factor is its outer shell (coverstock) and surface, which may be polished, sanded, solid, or pearl. The internal structure of the ball also affects how it behaves.

Polyester Plastic Balls. More advanced bowlers frequently use polyester plastic balls to make spares, because they do not hook (turn off their path) as easily as urethane balls or reactive balls. Plastic balls are also good for beginner bowlers. They are available at all bowling centers for your use. They can be purchased at a reasonable price at a bowling pro shop for you to own, and the pro shop will

drill holes in the ball to fit you. I do not recommend getting a bowling ball at a sports discount store; they usually do not have expert ball drillers, which can lead to many different problems.

Urethane Balls. A urethane ball will roll in an even way and will have a predictable reaction to the lane. It will give you a more powerful hit than a plastic ball. A urethane ball will give you less deflection (turning away of the ball when it hits the pins) and more pin carry than a plastic ball. (Pin carry means the ability of the ball to knock down pins.) Urethane balls can be drilled in different ways to give them the potential for different reactions on the lane. Urethane balls come in a variety of surfaces, suitable for different lane conditions.

Reactive Resin Balls. A reactive resin ball is a urethane ball with an additive in the coverstock (outer shell) that increases the friction (tackiness) between the lane and the ball's surface, increasing the hook potential of the ball so it will hook more and earlier than other balls. It also will react to the lane conditions more. On oil it will skid more; on dry lanes it will hook more. Reactive resin also gives a more powerful hit than urethane. Even though it is harder to control, it is the ball of choice of most better bowlers. Reactive resin balls come in solid or pearl surface. You can change the surface by either sanding or polishing it. In most cases, a pearl or polished surface is for dry lane conditions. A solid or sanded ball is for oily surface conditions.

A colorful plastic bowling ball.

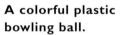

A urethane bowling ball.

Left: A solid reactive resin bowling ball.

A pearl reactive resin bowling ball.

Inside one type of bowling ball.

Equipment

A hand is measured for size.

Specifications are marked down.

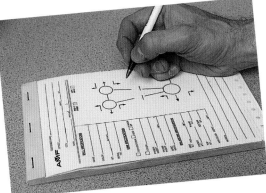

Fitting a Ball to You

To buy a bowling ball, it is important to go to a person who is skilled in fitting bowling balls to people's hands. The person should be IBPSIA certified if possible. IBPSIA stands for International Bowling Pro Shop & Instructors Association, Inc. IBPSIA-certified people are trained in this, and keep up with the latest developments. The holes are drilled to fit the bowler's fingers and thumb, as well as the span (the distance from the edge of the thumb hole nearest the center to the edge of a finger hole nearest the center) and the way the bowler wants to release the ball (grip).

Pitch, the angle that the axis (center line) of a finger hole or thumb hole makes in relation to a line through the geometric center of the ball, is also important in fitting.

Each of these measurements is different for each person. The ball needs to

A hole in a bowling ball being filled.

The hole is filled; the extra will be cut off. Then a new hole can be drilled.

Pitch of hole being checked with a pitch gauge.

A ball-drilling machine.

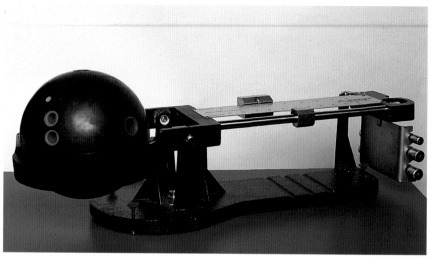

Scale for weighing a ball.

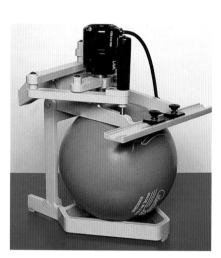

Engraving machine.

Coach Nace helps Fran with her grip.

be fitted to the person, so that it does not cause any injury to the hand. If you are getting any sores on your fingers or thumb, it is very possible that the ball fits your hand incorrectly. Get your grip checked. It is possible to have the holes in your ball

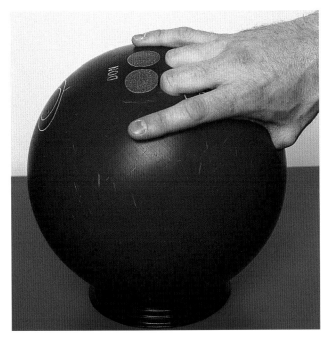

Conventional grip in a ball where the finger holes have been filled and redrilled.

Fingertip grip.

filled and have new holes redrilled correctly. If your ball driller cannot help you, go somewhere else.

If you are still growing, it is a good idea to get the ball's fit checked every 6 months, because your hand size changes just as the rest of you does. See page 70 for more information about bowling balls.

Grips

There are two different types of grip that are commonly used in bowling, conventional and fingertip. In the conventional grip, the holes are drilled deeply so that the fingers enter up to the second knuckle. In the fingertip grip, the fingers enter only up to the first knuckle. In all grips, the thumb must enter all the way into the hole. Entry-level bowlers usually use the conven-

tional grip. This is the grip used on all the balls that the bowling center supplies for your use. The more advanced bowler often prefers the fingertip grip. The fingertip grip encourages a quicker, smoother finger release than the conventional grip.

Resurfacing a Bowling Ball

A bowling ball can be resurfaced. After use, balls become dirty and have an area where the ball rolls most often, called a track. The track area gets many chips in it, which will affect the way the ball rolls down the lane. Other areas of the ball may get chips as well, and these can be removed most of the time by resurfacing the ball. This will help restore the ball's original surface. This would be done at a bowling pro shop.

Ball in need of resurface job.

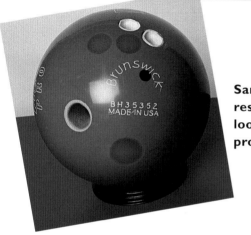

Same ball, resurfaced to look new in a pro shop.

Take good care of your bowling ball. Do not leave it in conditions of extreme heat or cold, such as in the trunk of a car, for long, or it may crack or break.

Inserts, Grips, and Slugs

Bowlers often have several balls that they use for different lane conditions. It is preferable, if you have more than one ball, for all of them to have the same feel. Even if you have one ball, finger grips and a thumb slug are recommended. There are inserts and solid slugs available for the thumb as well as the fingers, although finger solids are not often used by bowlers.

The purpose of the thumb insert and solid is to promote the same feel and smooth release when you change from ball to ball. Many people have oval thumbs, not round ones; therefore, thumb inserts can be round or oval. A solid has to be drilled to fit the thumb of the bowler. Finger grip inserts come in many different sizes, textures, and materials. As with the thumb inserts, finger inserts are used to give you a similar feel when using different balls. The result of all this fitting is to make the ball fit your hand like a glove. This will insure that you do not have to squeeze the ball to keep it from falling off your hand, and that it will not stay on your hand when it is supposed to come off. A bad fit can lead to sores on fingers or thumb, and even tendon problems in your arm.

Finger grip inserts will wear over time. They should be changed when this is evident, or every six months to a year, depending on how much you bowl.

Assorted finger and thumb grips.

Glove with wrist support.

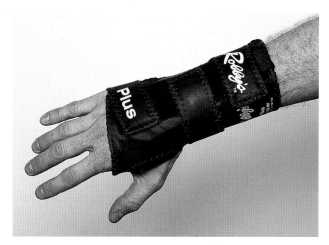
Wrist support.

Gloves and Wrist Supports

A glove and a wrist support for your bowling arm are other important pieces of equipment often needed by bowlers. Bowling gloves come with different style options. These include a tacky surface to help in gripping the ball, a firm device to help support the wrist, and a pad in the palm to help the thumb exit faster. Most common is a tacky glove or a tacky glove with wrist support.

Wrist supports can run from the fingers up the forearm. They help keep your hand in a straight, cupped, or cocked position. They usually have a firm support that runs on the back of the hand, with Velcro™ straps to hold them on. With some wrist supports, you are able to manually change the position of the wrist support; others don't move. Wrist supports are meant as training aids; they help you develop the feel that accompanies your release. Caution: A wrist support can become a crutch. Unless you have a medical reason for

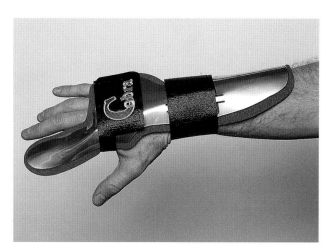
Wrist support that also keeps finger from bending back.

using one of these devices, it would be much better to develop your muscle strength and bowl without the device.

Shoes

Rental Shoes

A bowler needs specially designed shoes to help him or her bowl effectively. Bowling centers require you to use special shoes, which can be rented there.

Rental shoes.

Different styles of shoes you can purchase.

They aid your game and also protect the approach's surface.

A pair of shoes rented at a bowling center usually has both soles made of leather, and both heels of rubber, so they can be used by either right- or left-handed bowlers. They are harder to use than a pair of shoes that has one sliding sole and one traction sole. If you rent shoes at a bowling center, look for shoes that are one-half size smaller than your street shoes. Be sure you specify men's or women's shoes as the sizing is different for each.

Shoe with interchangeable soles and heels.

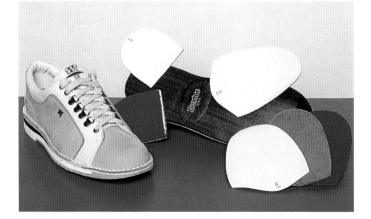

Buying Your Own Shoes

If you buy commercially made bowling shoes, you will be getting shoes that are fitted to you and take into account whether you are a right- or left-handed bowler. For a right-handed bowler, the right shoe has a sole with a lot of traction (gripping power), and the left shoe has a sole that slides easily. For a left-handed bowler, the right sole slides easily and the left sole has more traction. In other words, the sliding sole is on the opposite side to your bowling hand. You will need this sliding sole because the last step of your delivery, just as you let go of the ball, is a slide. Such shoes give you a much better start than rental shoes.

Low- to mid-priced shoes come in many different designs and colors; they can look like golf shoes, tennis shoes, or even wingtip dress shoes. The top of the line shoes are available in limited editions, and some can even accept interchangeable soles and heels, which are attached with Velcro.

Bag for balls and shoes.

Bag with wheels for balls and shoes.

Extras

You probably will need a towel to wipe the lane conditioning oil off your bowling ball after it has rolled down the lane. You may need some tape to put inside a bowling ball to adjust the width of the finger holes. Some bowlers use a rosin bag to absorb moisture on their hands before bowling. You might want to include a few plastic adhesive bandages and other first aid things for your hands in your bowling bag. A small wire brush for rubbing sticky things off the bottom of your shoes might come in handy. These things are all sold in a bowling pro shop.

Assorted accessories you should have in your bowling bag.

Chapter 4
The Basic 4-Step Delivery

Now that you understand some things about bowling etiquette and your equipment, you're ready to learn to roll a bowling ball. We will use the 4-step delivery. This is the most common delivery. It is the easiest way to achieve a free-flowing series of coordinated movements.

First we need some new words. The *delivery* includes the steps you take and the armswing you make from the start of the *stance* through to the *release* (letting go of the ball). Your *stance* means the way you stand at the start of your delivery.

The approach is the area on which you step while delivering the ball. The side of your body that has the hand you bowl with is your *swingside*. The foot on that side is your swingside foot. The arm opposite your bowling arm is called the *balance arm*. The foot you slide on is called your *sliding foot*.

General idea: You want your bowling arm to move like a pendulum. The weight of the ball moves it down and back. Your shoulder is the pivot of the pendulum. The elbow is locked when it swings. The wrist is firm. Don't try to hasten or slow the swing (an error known as muscling the ball). It's important to fit your footwork to your arm-swing, rather than the other way around. As you might guess from its name, in the 4-step delivery, you will be taking 4 steps, the last of which will be a slide.

On pages 38 and 39 we see a complete delivery and release. Now let's talk about it step by step.

Setup (Preshot Routine)

- Feet facing forward
- Knees straight
- Ball near chest, in line with swing-side shoulder and target (usually 2nd arrow from outside); wrist higher than elbow
- Weight of ball on balance hand, which is under bowling hand
- Keep head up

We have many things that can distract us when we are going up to bowl. It may be the noise from the bowling center. It could be our teammates or the team we are bowling against. We could put pressure on ourselves to get a strike, or think, "I really need to make this spare." To help deal with all these different distractions, you need to have a preshot routine. As individuals, we all have routines. You can develop one for bowling, one you repeat every time you bowl. Even if you are just practicing, it is important that you always follow the same routine.

(continued on page 40)

Wiping off your bowling ball might be part of your preshot routine.

Start of Step 1.

End of Step 1.

Step 2 starts.

Step 2 continues.

Step 3 begins.

Step 3.

Chris pulls his balance arm back as the ball moves forward, to gain power.

Here Chris moves his leg out of the way of the ball (Step 4).

The slide and the ball arrive at the foul line together.

Followthrough. Some people point at their target through and after release of the ball, as Chris does here.

Chris, in his stance.

Fran, in her stance.

(setup, continued)

For example, pick up your ball, wipe the ball off with a towel, put your hand over the air (there is always forced air by the ball return to dry your hand off), put your fingers in the ball, take a full breath as you get set on the approach, exhale, relax, and then start your delivery. A preshot routine takes your attention away from the things that distract you. You want to feel safe, positive, and focused on making a good shot, rather than focusing only on the strike or the spare. Before you pick up the ball or step on the approach, decide what you are going to shoot at and how you will do it. If at some time during the preshot routine something happens to stop you, put the ball down in the ball return and start over from the beginning.

Stance

Your stance is your position at the start of the delivery. It is important that you start at the same place on the approach every time. You are always looking for consistency — that is one of the most important things in bowling. Without it, you cannot make an intelligent adjustment of where to aim and release your ball. The elbow of the arm used for bowling should be against the side of your body at the start of the setup. In addition to your bowling hand being in the bowling ball, the opposite hand should hold the weight of the ball underneath. This helps rest the bowling arm a little. Most bowlers hold the ball waist high. It may be held chest level or below the waist as well, or anyplace

Coach Nace in his stance.

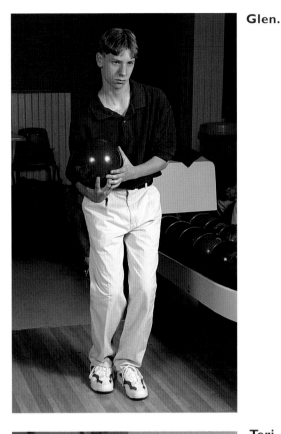

Glen.

Teri.

in between. The slower the delivery, the higher the ball should be held.

Where to Start

During your delivery, you are going to move up to the foul line and release the ball at the foul line, so you need to plan the correct distance for you. To find out how far back from the foul line to start, stand about 2 inches (5 cm) from the foul line with your back to the pins and take 4½ brisk steps away from the foul line. Then turn to face the pins. Then position yourself, using the guide dots on the boards to help you.

Right-handed bowler*:
First put the inside of your left foot on the center dot (board 20).

Left-handed bowler*:
First put the inside of your right foot on the center dot.

Right- or left-handed*:
Then place the other foot so the toes are aligned with the arch of the first foot, and the feet are about 2 inches (5 cm) apart.

*Note: These positions are for the first ball of the frame. For making a spare or split, see pages 58 to 67.

Keep the ball in line with your shoulder (top), not in the middle of your body.

Closeup of stance for right-handed bowler.

Closeup of stance for left-handed bowler.

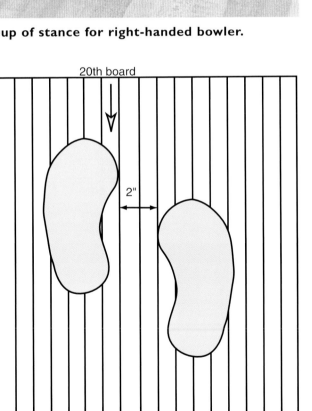

Righty: Starting position of feet for shooting strikes.

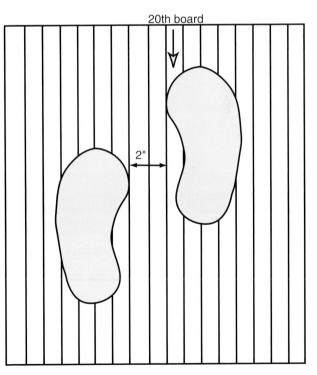

Lefty: Starting position of feet for shooting strikes.

Step 1, Fran.

Timing and coordination of arms and legs is crucial. It will help if you count from 1 to 4 while you do the following steps in the beginning.

Step 1

Arms: Extend bowling arm with ball straight out in front at the count of "1". Your balance arm supports the ball from underneath. Elbows are locked; wrist is firm. This is called the pushaway.

Feet: Step ahead in normal way on swingside foot so heel touches down at count of "1" — foot takes a normal stride.

Comments: When you extend your arm, move the ball straight out in front of you toward your target, not out to the right or left, which could send your arm and ball off target.

Step 2

Arms: The bowling arm with ball has moved down because of the weight of the ball, and is passing the swingside leg at the count of "2". Do not move your arm down; let the weight of the ball pull it down. Your balance hand moves shoulder high and even with the shoulder.

Feet: The heel of the balance side (sliding) foot touches down first, then the toe, in a normal stride for step 2, at the count of "2."

Comments: A right-handed bowler will let go of the ball with the left hand at the same time the left foot steps forward. For left-handed bowlers, the right hand will let go of the ball at the same time the right foot steps forward. At this point it is very important that the weight of the ball control the armswing.

The shoulder that is on the side of the ball should be in the direct line with your target. This may be the most important thing for getting the ball to hit what you are aiming at. Your arm should be free of all tension and you shouldn't be using any muscle. If you use muscle, your swing will not be the same at all times. When you are rested, it will be different than when you are tired. The best way to always have the same swing is to let the ball swing the arm. We are trying to achieve a consistent approach and swing.

Step 3

Arms: On the count of "3," the bowling arm has continued on its swing and the ball is now at top of backswing (the part of the swing that is behind your body). Then the ball starts to fall back, down from the top of its swing, with your fingers still in the holes, by its own weight.

Feet: On the count of "3," touch down the heel of your swingside foot first, then toes, on the approach to make the third step as an anchor for the slide to come.

Comments: The backswing should not move your shoulder out of the target line. Some bowlers bring their balls very high up in their backswing. This in itself is not bad, but it is harder to keep your shoulder in line with your target. If it moves out of the target line, it will have to be put back in line during your forward swing.

The height of the backswing should be the same all the time as well. You may think changing it a little means it is only 3 or 6 inches higher or lower, but that 3 or 6 inches really is doubled, because it happens on the second half of the swing also. If you do not bring your ball back behind you the proper distance, your timing is off — either early or late. This results in a loss of leverage or balance, which could cause you to miss your target or not get as much power in your shot as you should. Your shot execution also will not be consistent.

The beginning of Step 3.

Step 3 completed. The ball is now at the top of the backswing.

Step 4

Arms: At the count of "4," the arm holding the ball passes the swingside leg during its forward swing. Then it continues on straight out in front of you. Release the ball in an out-and-up manner. You don't want your arm to stop there. It should continue up above your head. Keep your eyes on the target.

Feet: Touch down with the sole of the sliding foot on the count of "4" and push it forward into the slide. Bend the leg of your sliding foot deeply. Let your hips move downward towards the floor. Your swingside leg extends behind your body, with the foot still on the floor.

Chris, at end of Step 4.

Body: Keep your back almost upright, maybe leaning forward a little, but keeping your torso in a "sitting tall" position. Keep eyes focused on target.

Comments: The arm should start down out of the backswing at the same time the sliding foot (balance side foot) starts forward. Remember: Don't use any arm muscle; the weight of the ball is in control.

The slide is done as the leg reaches the end of the fourth step. At this point the swingside leg should move in back of the sliding leg, and keep in contact with the approach; it should not be in the air. The sliding leg should be bent so your hips can be lowered to put you in a strong position. Your back should be bent a little forward. While you are in this position, the arm with the ball should continue through the arc, release the ball, and follow through. The arm will continue up above your head.

From the time you start your delivery until the time the ball leaves your hand, you should have one flowing motion. The muscles in your body are functioning as if in ballet, in one free-flowing series of movements. With the shoulder of the swingside arm in alignment with the target, the ball never leaves your target line. If you keep this target line, it will help compensate for many mistakes that might otherwise happen.

As the ball is released, it passes the knee of your swingside leg, the thumb comes out of the ball, the fingers are still in the holes, and the hand should continue to lift out and up.

Coach Nace's followthrough.

Fran's followthrough.

Followthrough

After the ball rolls off your hand and fingers, your arm will continue in its arc. Keep your shoulder and arm in the target line. Keep your sliding leg bent and your back bent a little forward.

It is important to maintain this position. Standing up, bending forward, and leaning to the side are things that will take you out of the strong position. That will take you out of your target line, which will make you miss your target.

Remember the board on which you put your balance side foot in the stance?

(For the right-handed bowler that is the left foot, and for the left-handed bowler, the right foot.) After you have released the ball, look down at your sliding foot. It should be on the same board as it was in your stance. If it is right or left by more than 2 boards, that could cause you to miss your target.

Arm and Hand Positions

Your arm should be kept close to your body from the stance until the ball is off your hand. If your elbow moves out away from your side, your hand will go to the top of the ball, losing power in your shot. You will not get good leverage on the ball. It is very likely that you will miss your target as well.

It is very important that you maintain good balance throughout your delivery and at the finish position. Bending too far forward, standing straight up, leaning from one side to the other, a twisting motion, or falling after the slide are all indications of bad balance. You must execute your shot from a stable position.

On pages 50 and 51 we see the back view of the 4-step delivery.

Stance.

The ball and leg move forward together.

Step 1.

Left leg and ball move forward together.

Step 2; the ball beside the leg.

The ball keeps moving back as your right leg moves forward.

The ball is at the highest point of the backswing (end of Step 3).

Moving down (beginning of Step 4).

The right leg moves out of the way for the ball to get by.

Ball release is beside foot. Maintain your balance as you begin the followthrough.

Maintain your position until the ball hits the pins.

Here is how the sequence would look for a left-handed person. Logan is bowling lefty here.

Stance.

Step 1.

Letting go of the ball with the nonbowling hand at the start of Step 2.

The start of Step 2 continues. Nonbowling arm starts to go to the side for balance.

Step 2 finished; ball beside his leg.

Start of Step 3

Step 4 starts.

The ball and sliding foot move forward together.

Keep your balance through release of the ball.

Followthrough.

Hands at Release — Strike Shot

By the time you reach the point of release, the ball should be in a straight line in front of your elbow and shoulder. If someone is standing behind you, he would see just a little of the ball during the setup of the delivery. The position of your hand at release with a 90° rotation is as if you were going to shake hands with someone.

Another way to look at your hand position at release is to imagine the face of a clock around the bowling ball. A right-handed bowler's ring finger should be at the 5 o'clock position at the release for a 45° rotation. A left-handed bowler's ring finger should be at 7 o'clock.

The wrist should be straight, and should be kept that way until the ball is off your hand. This is sometimes hard to do, because of the strength of your wrist and forearm. It is still very important and worth the effort to try to do this.

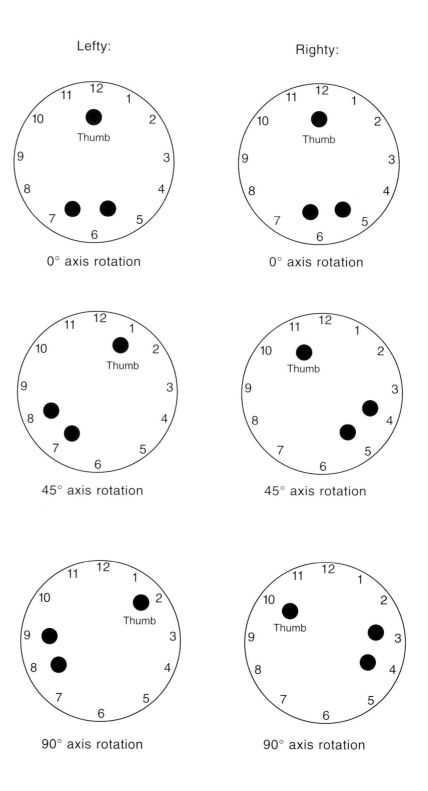

Lefty:

0° axis rotation

45° axis rotation

90° axis rotation

Righty:

0° axis rotation

45° axis rotation

90° axis rotation

For lefty: Top to bottom: 0°, 45°, and 90° axis rotation, using clock face as guide.

For righty: Top to bottom: 0°, 45°, and 90° axis rotation, using clock face as guide.

Chapter 5
Strikes, Spares, and Splits

When you knock down all 10 pins with the first ball you throw in a frame, it is called a strike.

Strikes

The strike shot most people try to make starts by placing the first (sliding) foot on the same board as the center dot of the approach (the 20th board). Then you aim at the 2nd to 3rd arrow in from the outside of the lane. Right-handers count arrows from the right. Left-handers count arrows from the left. It is much easier to aim at the arrows, which are 15 feet (4.57 m) away, than to aim at the pins 60 feet (18 m) away.

Righty: Strike shot, aiming between the 2nd and 3rd arrow from right.

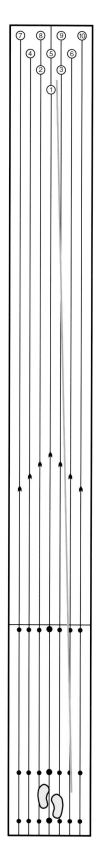

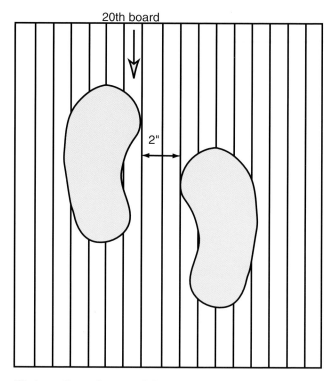

20th board

2"

Righty: Starting position of feet for shooting strikes.

If your ball hits your target arrow on the lane, but misses the pin to the right, the adjustment you make is to move your feet right a few boards. Aim at the same target on the lane as before. If the ball misses the pin to the left, you move to the left with your feet. How much should you move? A move of one board on the approach equals two boards at the pins, two boards on the approach equal 4 boards at the pins, and so on. We will return to this in more detail later.

Lefty: Strike shot, aiming between the 2nd and 3rd arrow from left.

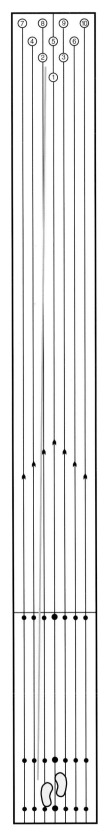

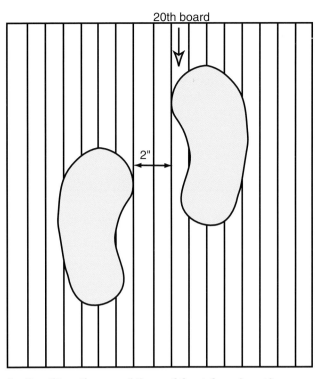

Lefty: Starting position of feet for shooting strikes.

The pocket is the most desirable location for the ball to hit the pins in order to maximize chances of getting a strike. For the right-handed bowler it is usually between the #1 and #3 pins. For the left-handed player it is between the #1 and #2 pins.

If you are getting the ball to the pocket and are still not getting a strike, move your feet one or two boards right or left on the approach, or move your target a board or two right or left. Do not get stuck, thinking, "I am hitting the pocket, and sometimes I get a strike." If you are hitting the pocket and not getting a strike, you're in the wrong spot. Most of us have a hard time moving when we are hitting the pocket, but the one that makes the move is the one that will win the game.

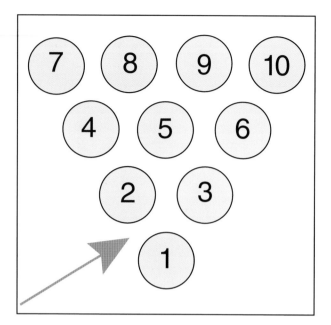

Pocket for lefty.

Pocket for righty.

Spares

When the second ball you roll in a frame knocks down all the pins that the first ball didn't knock down, it is called a spare. Most people do not practice making spares enough, because it is so much fun practicing strikes, but spares win or lose more games than strikes do. You should practice making spares so that you become familiar with how to make them; then, when you have to make them in a game, you will be more confident. A split is a spare setup of pins in which the remaining pins have one or more pins down between them, in any direction.

The 2–4–5 spare.

Possible target pins, for target pin method of making spares.

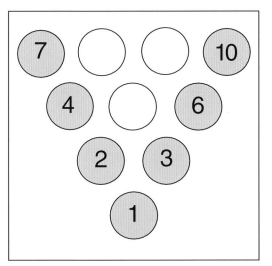

Target pin is #2, if #2 and #4 are standing.

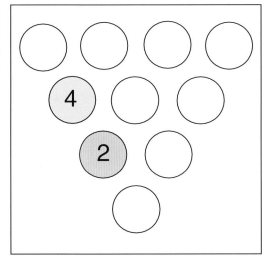

Target pin is #6, if #9 and #10 are standing.

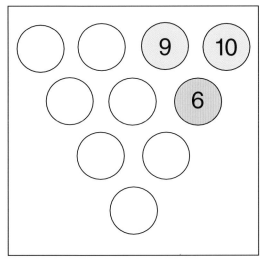

Target Pin Method for Spares

Many people have no idea what to do when trying to make a spare; they just throw the ball and hope the ball hits the pins. Using the concept of target pins, you can take the mystery out of spare shots and split shots. With this system, there are only seven different spare shots you have to know, although there are many different pin combinations that may be left standing. The seven different target pins are the outside pins of the pin triangle: the #1, 2, 3, 4, 6, 7, and 10 pins.

You decide what to aim at to make your spare by looking for the pin that is the closest to you; that will usually be your target pin.

Example: #2 and #4 pins are standing. The #2 pin is the target pin.

Example: #9 and #10 pins are standing. The #6 pin is the target pin, even though it is not standing.

The 9–10 spare. Aim at the #6 pin.

Example: If the #4 and #5 pin are standing, shoot at the #2 pin.

This system of spare- and split-making can only work if you are consistent with your delivery, armswing, and the release of your ball. This happens after you know where you are going to stand on the approach and what spot you are aiming at on the lane to make strikes.

If you are standing at the center dot and aiming at the 3rd arrow from the outside for your strike shot, your spare and split shots will be based on that position. When you are shooting straight up the lane, your shoulders will be perpendicular to your target at the moment you release the ball. When you move right with your feet and still aim at the middle of the lane, you must turn your shoulders left. If you move your feet left, you must turn your shoulders right to keep your target alignment.

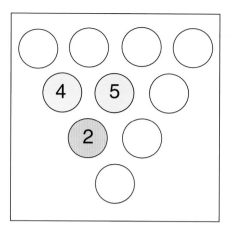

Target pin is #2 if #4 and #5 are standing.

This turn of your shoulders right or left is very little. You must still walk straight up to the foul line. For example, if you start with your sliding foot on the 10th board, you must finish with your sliding foot on the 10th board.

Below are some examples of where to stand, and where to aim your ball to make spares. Release the ball in the same way you would release your first ball of the frame.

Right-Handed Bowler — Target Pin Method of Spares

Spare Pin Target	Where to Place Left Foot	Aim
#1 or 5 pin	Left foot on 20th board	3rd arrow
#2 or 8 pin	3 boards right of 20th board	3rd arrow
#4 pin	6 boards right of 20th board	3rd arrow
#7 pin	9 boards right of 20th board	3rd arrow
#3 or 9 pin	4 boards left of 20th board	2 boards left of 3rd arrow
#6 pin	8 boards left of 20th board	4 boards left of 3rd arrow
#10 pin	12 boards left of 20th board	6 boards left of 3rd arrow

Left-Handed Bowler — Target Pin Method of Spares

Spare Pin Target	Where to Place Right Foot	Aim
#1 or 5 pin	Right foot on 20th board	3rd arrow from left
#2 or 8 pin	4 boards right of 20th board	2 boards right of 3rd arrow from left
#4 pin	8 boards right of 20th board	4 boards right of 3rd arrow from left
#7 pin	12 boards right of 20th board	6 boards right of 3rd arrow from left
#3 or 9 pin	3 boards left of 20th board	3rd arrow from left
#6 pin	6 boards left of 20th board	3rd arrow from left
#10 pin	9 boards left of 20th board	3rd arrow from left

Note: There are other things you can do to increase your chances of making a spare. They are things that keep your ball rolling straight, avoiding hooking. In general, things that decrease friction will decrease hooking.

1. Increase speed of delivery. If other things are equal, a faster ball will hook less than a slow ball.
2. Get bowling ball polished.
3. Use a hard-shell ball.
4. Change your grip so your ring finger (in the ball) is at about 6 o'clock instead of being at 5 or 4 o'clock (righties); or at 6 o'clock instead of being at 7 or 8 o'clock (lefties).

Straight Shot Method of Making Spares

This is another system that is very good for making spares. In this method, for your spare shots, you only have two targets, one for the pins on the right side of the head pin (#1 pin) and one for the pins on the left side of the head pin. This will help get you into a comfort zone. When you feel comfortable, it is easier to hit the target you are aiming at. You will be able to release the ball so that it will go straight with no hook. With your ball going straight, you do not have to worry about whether lane conditions are dry or oily. Where you aim the ball will always be the same.

Right-Handed Bowler: Straight Shot Method of Making Spares: #10 Pin Is Starting Pin

Move left foot to right from 40th board:	To hit this pin:
3 boards	#6 pin
6 boards	#3 pin
6 boards	#9 pin

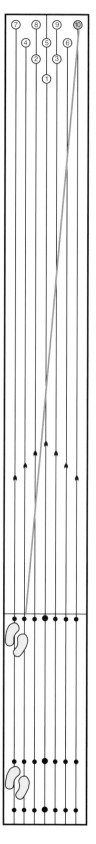

For righty: Straight shot method of making spares to right of the head pin, targeting #10 pin.

Right-Handed Bowler: Straight Shot Method of Making Spares

For pins on the right side of the head pin, a right-handed bowler starts with the left foot on about the 40th board and aims for the #10 pin, which means aiming between the 3rd and 4th arrow (15th to 20th boards). Keep good shoulder alignment, and the ball must go straight. It may take a few tries to find the right spot to stand, and the right target board for the ball to roll over. After you get it, this will always be the same no matter what the condition of the lane. The ball will not be affected by whether the lane is dry or oily. Now that you know where to stand and aim at for the #10 pin, move your feet right the correct number of boards as indicated above to make the other spares.

You are aiming at the same spot on the lane for all these pins, between the 3rd and 4th arrows. When you move your feet right, your right shoulder will turn left a very small amount. The target on the lane is what you are aiming at, not the pin. Getting the pin down is the result of hitting the target on the lane.

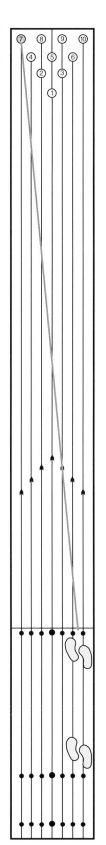

For righty: Straight shot method of making spares to the left of the head pin, targeting the #7 pin.

Right-Handed Bowler: Straight Shot Method of Making Spares: #7 Pin Is Starting Pin

Move left foot to left from 10th board:	To hit this pin:
3 boards	#4 pin
6 boards	#2 pin
6 boards	#8 pin
9 boards	#1 pin
9 boards	#5 pin

For the pins on the left side of the head pin, the #7 pin is the starting pin for righties. Start with your left foot around the 10th board, and aim at the 3rd arrow. After you find the position of where to stand and what target to aim at, move your feet left the correct number of boards as indicated above to make the other spares.

For the #1 and #5 pin, you can use the same delivery as if you were rolling your first ball.

Left-Handed Bowler: Straight Shot Method of Making Spares: #7 Pin Is Starting Pin

Move right foot to left from 40th board from left:	To hit this pin:
3 boards	#4 pin
6 boards	#2 pin
6 boards	#8 pin

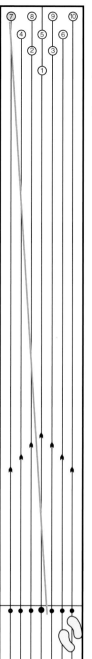

For lefty: Straight shot method of making spares to left of head pin, targeting #7 pin.

Left-Handed Bowler: Straight Shot Method of Making Spares

If you are a left-handed bowler, the starting position with this method is with the right foot on about the 40th board from the left, while you aim at the #7 pin to make spares to the left of the head pin. Looking at the arrows, you always aim at the 3rd to 4th arrows from the left (15th to 20th boards from the left). Move your feet left the correct number of boards, as indicated above, to make the other spares. Remember, a right-handed bowler counts from the right side of the lane, and a left-handed bowler counts from the left side of the lane. In this method, you release the ball straight with no hook. After you find your position, you adjust to hit the different pins by moving your feet, but always aim for the same spot, the 3rd to 4th arrows from the left.

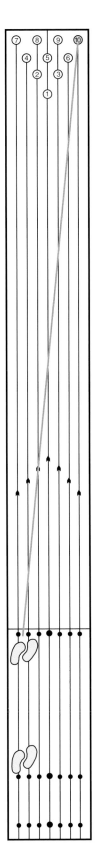

Left-Handed Bowler: Straight Shot Method of Making Spares: #10 Pin Is Starting Pin

Move right foot to the right from 10th board from left:	To hit this pin:
3 boards	#6 pin
6 boards	#3 pin
6 boards	#9 pin
9 boards	#1 pin
9 boards	#5 pin

For the pins on the right side of the head pin, the pin you will be aiming at is the #10 pin. You will be aiming at around the 3rd arrow from the left. Your starting position is with the right foot on the 10th board from the left. Move your feet right the correct number of boards, as indicated above, to make other spares.

These are not the only methods of shooting spares, but they both are very good. Some bowlers like one better than the other. Whatever method you prefer, that should be the one you use. At some point you may change to the other system, so practice both ways so you are able to use either one.

The 3–10 split. Aim at the #6 pin.

The 2–7 split. Aim at the #4 pin.

Splits

A split is a spare setup of pins in which the remaining pins have one or more pins down between them. To make a split, you will again shoot off your strike line (start from your strike position). As in the examples shown below, for many splits you will shoot at a pin that is not actually standing. The ball will hit the side of the pin you need to hit, however.

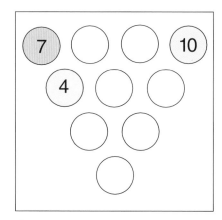

Split: Target pin is #7 if #4 and #10 pin are standing.

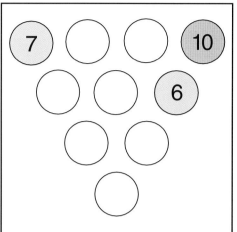

Target pin is #10 if #6 and #7 pin are standing.

Examples of Splits and Pins to Aim For

Pins Left Standing	Pin to Aim For
4–10 split	#7 pin
6–7 split	#10 pin
3–10 split	#6 pin
2–7 split	#4 pin
1–2–10 split	#2 pin
1–3–8 split	#2 pin

Chapter 6
More About Bowling Balls and Lane Conditions

The way a ball reacts to the lane is based on many things. The bowler's delivery influences the speed, as well as the way the ball rotates around itself and moves down the lane. The material of the ball itself — whether polyester, urethane, or reactive resin — also makes a difference. The ball's surface or shell is an important factor. It may be polished, sanded, solid, or pearl. The internal ball contributes to the effect by its structure also.

In addition, the location and amount of lane conditioning oil on the lanes affects how the ball reacts. When you bowl after conditioning oil is applied, you will find different conditions on the lane's surface than before. The lane may be oily in the middle and dry in the back, dry in the front and oily in the back, oily in the middle of the lane and dry on the sides, or dry in the middle and oily on the sides. (Conditioner is not applied to the approach, the area before the foul line.)

Lane Conditions: Be a Detective

What can you do to adapt to this? Start in the position in which you feel most comfortable, at the spot on the lane that is best for you. You will need to be a bit of a detective to figure out what the lane conditions are. In other sports, you can see what the conditions are. For example, in golf, you can see trees, sand traps, water holes, and other hazards. Bowl awhile and watch your ball travel down the lane. It will skid, hook, and then roll. Skidding means the ball is moving forward without rotating.

If the ball skids a long way, the front of the lane is oily. If it does not skid very far, the front is dry in the part of the lane you used. (To the right or left, conditions may be different.) If the ball does not hook and roll toward the pins, there is oil in the back of the lane. If the ball hooks a lot, the back end of the lane is dry. (To the right or left of the spot you bowled from, conditions could be different, however.)

If you understand these factors, you can start to control them and adapt your game and your equipment to them.

BOWLING BALL ANATOMY

In selecting a ball and rolling it, you have many choices. Surface is very important, and there are other things that need to be considered. The construction of the bowling ball affects how it will behave. The following are some other terms you may see on a bowling ball, with general explanations of each.

Coverstock. The coverstock is the outer coating of the ball. Many experts agree that the coverstock or surface is the most important part of ball choice. One way to characterize coverstock is by the terms highly aggressive, aggressive, and mellow. Highly aggressive (high-friction coverstock) is used for oily lane conditions and fast ball speed; aggressive is for average conditions and medium ball speed; and mellow (lowest friction) is for dry conditions and slow ball speed.

Coefficient of Friction: Friction is the force that resists the motion of one surface in relation to another surface with which it is in contact. Surfaces, even smooth ones, resist motion, but rough surfaces resist more than smooth ones. The coefficient of friction is a measure of how much a surface resists movement. The higher the coefficient of friction, the more the surface resists movement. A rough surface might have a coefficient of friction of 1.5; a smooth surface, .001. Bowling ball surfaces are designed to have various coefficients of friction, depending on the conditions they will be used in. The higher the coefficient of friction, the better suited the ball is to oily conditions. Friction helps slow the ball down so it can change direction and hook toward the pins. The lower the coefficient of friction, the better the ball is for dry lanes.

Surface. You can change the way the ball will react by changing the surface of the ball by polishing or sanding it. Polish decreases friction and will help the ball get farther down the lane before it begins to roll. This will also delay hooking. Sanding increases friction and will make the ball roll and hook sooner. A surface with more friction (solid or sanded) is better for oily lane conditions. Using a surface with less friction (polished or pearl) is good for dry lane conditions.

Bowling Ball Materials

Plastic (polyester) balls are frequently used for making spares, when people want the ball to roll straight, because they don't hook as easily as urethane or reactive resin balls.

Urethane balls roll in an even and pre-dictable way, but have less deflection (are turned off course less by hitting the pins) and have more pin carry (they knock down more pins) than a poly-ester ball.

Reactive resin balls have an additive in the coverstock that increases the friction (tackiness) between the lane and the ball's sur-face, so it will hook more and earlier than other balls. A reactive resin ball also reacts more easily to lane con-ditions than other balls do. On oil, it will skid more; on dry lanes it will hook more. It is harder to control but gives a more powerful hit than urethane.

Axis of rotation. The center of all circular paths on a rigid object that is rotating is called the axis of rota-tion. On a bowling ball, it is an imaginary line, perpendicular to the track, around which a bowling ball rotates during its path down the lane.

Preferred spin axis (PSA): The axis about which the bowling ball wants to rotate.

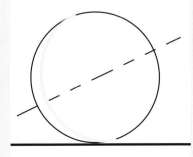

Axis of rotation (dashed line) is perpendicular to the ball's path (blue line).

Radius of gyration (RG): The radius of gyration is the distance from the axis of rotation at which the mass (weight) of a bowling ball effectively is located. The RG affects how fast a ball rotates. Picture an ice skater turning a pirouette: when her arms are out she goes more slowly than when her arms are tucked in. More of her weight is towards the inside when her arms are in, and her radius of gyration is decreased. The way the weight inside the bowling ball is arranged, and also its cover, affects its RG. Bowling balls are rated as to RG. A low RG ball is center-heavy, and a ball with a high RG is cover-heavy. Minimum and maximum standards on RG are set by the ABC/WIBC. The minimum cannot be less than 2.430 inches from the axis of rotation and the maximum cannot be more than 2.8 inches. A low RG ball is said to roll more easily than a high RG ball. For this reason, it is good to use a low RG ball for oily conditions and a high RG ball for dry lane conditions.

Differential: The differential is the difference between the lowest and highest possible RG you can get with a particular ball, depending on how it is drilled. Differential is an indication of track flare potential. The maximum allowable differential according to the ABC/WIBC is .080. Differentials of .01 or .02 mean the ball has low track flare potential; .05 to .08 mean a ball has a high track flare potential. The more the track flare potential, the earlier the ball will hook and roll. Large differential balls are used for oily lanes, and small differential for dry lanes.

Track flare: Track flare refers to the bowling ball's changing its axis of rotation from the axis it had when it was released, while seeking its preferred spin axis during its path down the lane. A new ball surface touches the lane on each revolution. If there is oil on the lanes, you can see a record of this by looking at the several distinct oil rings around the ball. A large flare can be 7 inches (18 cm) from the first ring to the last one. A small flare may be 2 inches (5 cm) from the first to last; sometimes the rings may even be on one line.

Track flare potential is the maximum amount the axis of the ball can migrate, given its construction, but it is also dependent on the release of the bowler. A ball with higher flare potential generally is better for oily lane conditions. A ball with small flare potential is better for dry conditions. The higher the flare, the earlier the ball will roll, and the sooner it will hook.

Your Delivery

Each person has a unique way of throwing a ball, including the speed, revolutions, axis rotation, and tilt that he or she puts on a ball at release.

Speed. A fast ball speed is needed for dry lanes and a slow one for oily lanes. You need to be able to roll the ball with smooth contact with the lanes, or loft it in the air onto the lanes. Speed is generated by the bowler.

Revolutions. Revolutions are the number of times your ball turns around itself as it rolls down the lane. A lot of revolutions with a slow ball speed may cause the ball to hook (turn inward off its path) too early. With a lot of speed but few revolutions, the ball may not hook. Revolutions are given to the ball by the bowler's hand on releasing the ball.

Axis rotation. Axis rotation refers to where your fingers are at the release of the ball. Hold the ball in front of you with your fingers in it and pretend the ball is the face of a clock. For right-handers: If your two fingers in the ball are at 6 o'clock to 5 o'clock, that is considered low rotation. If they are at 5 to 4 o'clock, that is medium rotation. If they are at 4 to 3 o'clock that is high rotation. For left-handers: If your two fingers in the ball are at 6 to 7 o'clock, that is low rotation. If they are at 7 to 8 o'clock, that is medium rotation. If they are at 8 to 9 o'clock, that is high rotation.

Low rotation is good for oily lanes. Medium rotation is good for medium lanes, and high rotation is good for dry lanes.

Fingers at 4 to 3 o'clock, high rotation release.

Axis tilt. Axis tilt is determined by the position of your wrist when you release the ball. Axis tilt helps keep the ball from deflecting and helps improve pin carry. If you are a right-handed bowler getting a good hit and your ball is deflecting, leaving the #8 pin, you may need more axis tilt. If you are getting a good hit and the ball is going through the pins, but leaving the #9 pin, you may have too much axis tilt. For a left-handed bowler, if you are leaving the #8 pin you may need less axis tilt. If you are leaving the #9 pin, you may need more axis tilt.

Bowler's Qualities and Ball Choice

Below is a list of some qualities you may have, and what ball choice may be good for you in general. If you have:

High ball speed: Use a ball with low RG core, higher differential, high flair potential, highly aggressive coverstock. You may have to sand the surface of the ball to get it into a forward roll.

Low ball speed: Use a ball with high RG core, low differential, low flare potential, pearl cover; surface may need polishing.

90° axis rotation: Use a ball with low RG, low differential core.

45° axis rotation: Use a ball with medium RG core, low differential core, pearl coverstock.

Few revolutions: Use a ball with high differential core, highly aggressive coverstock; low RG.

Many revolutions: Use a ball with low differential core, pearl coverstock, high RG core.

Chapter 7
Straight Shots, Hook Shots, and Finding the Strike Spot

O nce you see what the lane conditions are, it is up to you to make your decision as to how you will play the lanes. Will you move on the approach, aim at a different spot on the lane, or change the way you deliver the ball?

It is best if you can change your axis tilt, axis rotation, revolution or speed, as well as how far out on the lane you are releasing the ball — close to or far away from the foul line. These changes may help your pin carry and also may make your bowling more versatile under different lane conditions.

Don't Fight the Lanes

Oily lanes. Do not try to fight the lanes. You will not win. If the lane is oily and your ball is not hooking, play a straighter game. If you try harder to make the ball hook, it could go straighter. Think of tires on ice trying to turn. The more you try to turn, the worse it gets. Then if you do hit a dry spot, you will get too much of a hook.

If the lanes are oily, a right-handed bowler would move to the right if he sees that the ball is not getting to the strike pocket. A left-handed bowler would move to the left. Roll the ball off your hand with less speed, setting it down at the foul line or even before the foul line. Aim in a direct manner toward the pocket. You would release at a 45° rotation on your ball.

Dry lanes. If the lane is dry, your ball will hook easily. A right-handed bowler would move left when he sees the ball is hooking too much in the pocket. A left-handed bowler would move right. You would aim your ball more toward the sides of the lane to give it more room to move back to the pocket.

There are times the lane may be too dry, and you have too much hook. At this time you should play a straight game. (See p.54 for diagrams of rotation.) For a straight game you would use 0° of axis rotation.

Release

Most bowlers have a release that is natural to them, and you probably do, too. Whether it is a 0°, 45°, or 90° axis rota-tion, you think of this as your game. You should practice other releases also, so you can be versatile in dealing with different lane conditions you may encounter. The 45° rotation is the best all around. Zero rotation is for oily or very dry conditions. A rotation of 90° is used when the back part of the lane is dry. With 0° of axis rotation, a ball will roll very soon with very little hook. With 45° of axis rotation, the ball will skid, then hook, and roll in the back of the lane. With 90° of axis rotation, the ball will skid the longest distance and hook with a snap at the back of the lane, and then roll.

The Straight Shot

The straight shot is a very good release to use if the lanes are hooking a lot, and for making single pin spares. To do the straight shot, have your wrist in a relaxed position (wrist bent back), with gripping fingers behind the ball at the 6 o'clock position from the time you line up in your stance until you release the ball. Your arm swings like a pendulum and your elbow bend is perpendicular to your armswing (parallel to the foul line). Be careful not to turn your hand to the side of the ball at the release, which could make the ball hook.

Do not throw the ball so hard that you lose your accuracy. If you are using a plastic (polyester) ball, it will go straight. If you are using a ball that will normally hook, it may still hook just a little.

The Hook Shot

A hook shot rolls a ball that follows a bent path to the pins from the bowler's outside (swingside) to the inside. The ball rolls down the lane and at the breakpoint makes a change in direction and starts to hook.

You need side rotation (45° to 90° of axis rotation) and revolution on the ball for a hook shot. You may use a ball with the most hook potential drilled for the most hook, but you have to put rotation and revolutions on the ball with your release, or it will not hook. The easiest way to do this is to hold your wrist in a cupped or strong position with your gripping fingers on the side of the ball at about 4 to 5 o'clock from your setup to the release of the ball. For a lefty, the gripping fingers would be at 7 to 8 o'clock. This will give you a medium amount of hook.

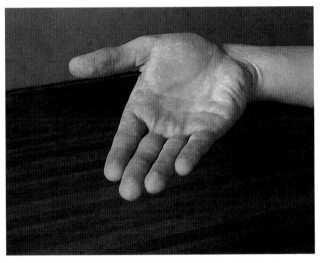

Cocking the wrist for axis tilt.

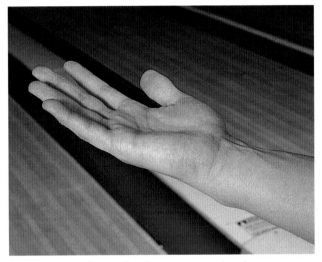

Use a straight wrist for a normal release.

Use a cupped wrist to help the ball hook.

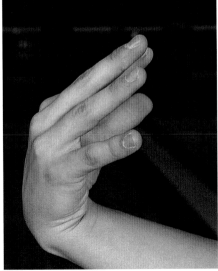

A relaxed wrist will help the ball go straight.

A second way to do a hook shot is to have your wrist go from a cupped position in the setup until the moment of release, when your wrist goes to a relaxed position. This will put revolutions on the ball and put your fingers on the side of the ball. If you do not put side rotation on the ball, the ball will not hook. The faster you go from cupped to a relaxed position, the more revs (revolutions) will be put on the ball. You do not want your fingers to go any more to the side of the ball than the 3 o'clock position. The most versatile position is 4 to 5 o'clock for a righty and 7 to 8 o'clock for a lefty.

Many bowlers try to "help" the ball hook. It is not good to pull the arm to the right or left in the release. You should follow through straight out and up. Make a decision as to where the ball will be released and do that. Once you make a decision, stick to it. In bowling we say: "Believe in the shot." Never second-guess yourself. When you do not believe in the delivery, you have many different things running through your mind, which will just lead to confusion in releasing the ball.

Releasing the ball in the cupped position will help the ball to hook. If it is not going far enough down the lane before it begins to hook, you may want to put your hand in a cupped position, at the same time cocking the wrist to the side. You would release the ball the same as in the cupped position. At the bottom of your swing, your hand would go from the cocked and cupped position to relaxed. The armswing is still out on the lane, not in an up manner.

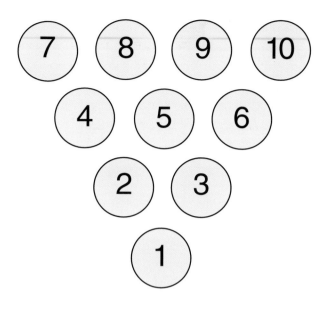

Because lane conditions vary, you need to adapt your game to the conditions you find. This includes finding the strike spot.

Finding the Strike Spot
Right-Handed Bowler

Take some practice shots. Start by aiming at the #7 pin. If the ball does not get to the #7 pin, and misses to the right, you know that the back of the lane is oily in that area. If the ball misses left, going in the channel, you know that the back of the lane is dry in that area. Then aim at the #10 pin. If your ball misses to the right, you know that area in the back of the lane is oily. If the ball misses to the left, you know that area of the lane in the back is dry. Then aim at the #2 pin. If your ball misses right, you know that the middle of the lane is oily. If it misses left, you know that the middle of the lane is dry.

Left-Handed Bowler

Start by aiming at the #10 pin. If the ball does not get to the #10 pin and misses to the left, the back part of the lane is oily in that area. If the ball misses right, and goes into the channel, the back part of the lane is dry. The next pin to aim for is the #7 pin. If the ball misses left of the #7 pin, the back part of the lane is oily. If the ball misses right of the #7 pin, the back part of the lane is dry. The next pin to aim for is the #3 pin. If you miss left of the pin, the middle of the lane is oily. If you miss right of the pin, the middle of the lane is dry.

The strike shot would be next. From the first three shots you rolled, you see the condition of the lane. You will have a good idea of where to stand on the approach, and where to aim your ball. You may still have to make small

adjustments with your feet, as well as to where you aim the ball for your strike shot. As the game goes on, especially in league play, if there are four bowlers on a team, there could be as many as fourteen balls traveling down the lane before your next turn on that lane. This will change the conditions of the lane. You must be watching this all the time. Watch your ball as it travels down the lane. Watch for a change in the way it skids, hooks, rolls, and where it hits the pins. This way you can make adjustments to where you are standing and where you are throwing the ball to keep your ball in the strike pocket.

The Heads

Does the ball skid a shorter distance on the first part of the lane than before? If so, the front part of the lane is drying out. This will make the ball hook sooner than before. You need to adjust to this to keep the ball in the pocket. There are different adjustments. You could move your target left or maybe right to find oil so the ball will skid just as far again. You can change your hand to a more relaxed position, causing the ball to skid farther. You might change to a ball that has a more polished surface, as a polished ball skids a longer distance than a duller ball. You can also loft the ball out on the lane.

The Hook Area

Let's say the ball gets through the front part of the lane (the heads) well. The next part of the lane is the middle part,

You will leave corner pins because of this. You may also leave splits or what is called solid eights or nines.

The Back End of the Lane

In the past, before the more aggressive bowling balls we have today, there was a condition called "carrydown," where the ball would move the oil down the lane to the back end. The balls of today absorb the oil; they do not carry it down the back end. Because of carrydown, the ball would not be able to hook toward the pins. Carrydown may still happen, but what will most likely happen is that the middle part of the lane will become dry, causing the ball to hook out sooner and then go into a roll sooner. If you are not watching for this, you may be thinking the ball is not hooking at the end of the lane. You may think that there is oil in the back part of the lane and that this is why the ball is not hooking in. If this is the problem, you may need to go to a ball that has a less aggressive coverstock. If you are using a sanded ball, go to a pearl or polished ball, or maybe more speed is needed. You have to watch your ball to see what it is doing. If you don't realize this, you may adjust as if the backend is oily, which will only make things worse.

known as the pines. This is the hook area. If the ball is hooking more than it did before, it is possible that the pines is drying out. If this is a problem, move your target left or right. Use a ball with a polished surface or a ball that does not flare as much to help get more distance from your ball. Rolling the ball into the pocket is very important. You do not want your ball hooking when it makes contact with the pins. A ball that is hooking is also skidding, and if it is skidding the ball will deflect (turn aside), rather than drive into the pins.

Chapter 8
Troubleshooting

Drifting, bad balance, and missing the target to the right or left usually are problems caused by bad training. All of us know how to walk and swing our arms as we walk, but put a bowling ball in our hands and it seems we can't walk anymore. When approaching the foul line, some run, some walk, others skip, and still others take very small steps. The right delivery is 4 or 5 steps, then a slide. The bowling ball should swing freely at your side. You must bowl in a natural way for you, whatever that may be. Do not look at someone else's delivery and think, "What a nice, high backswing,"

and then try to imitate that. It would be alright only if it is natural for you. If you have to force the backswing or any part of your delivery, don't do it.

Timing

For the 4-step delivery, the ball will start to move on your first step. If you start the ball at the correct time in your approach to the foul line, it will be much easier to be free of tension in your arm as well as in your body, and most timing problems will disappear. Timing may be early or late, which refers to the ball. "Early" means that the ball is at the finish of the delivery before the sliding foot. "Late" means that your sliding foot is at the finish before the ball.

Timing starts with your stance. When you are in your stance, if your upper body is too far back, too straight, the ball will be ahead of you and your timing will be too early. When your upper body is too far forward, the ball will arrive after you; that is late timing. If your timing is off, either early or late, you will not be in a good position for leverage. Leverage means getting most power out of your release. You do not have to force this. When your timing and balance position are good, you will get the most leverage without even trying.

During the first step of a 4-step delivery, many timing problems occur. For a right-handed person, the ball and the right foot move at the same time on the first step. For a left-handed person, the ball and the left foot move together.

The pushaway with the ball should be straight out in front — out and down, not up. You can adjust your timing by changing the position in which you hold the ball during your stance, when you first start. If the speed of your delivery is slow, hold the ball higher in the stance. If your delivery is too fast, hold the ball lower in the stance. Your back-swing height should not be changed. It may be different from one person to another. Whatever is natural for you, it must be constant. Be aware that swinging too high a backswing would result in late timing; a too low back-swing would result in early timing.

Adjusting the ball height in your stance can help your timing.

Early and Late Timing Problems

Early Timing Problems

Right-handed bowler: The ball misses its target to the left.

Right-handed bowler: You drift to the right.

Left-handed bowler: The ball misses its target to the right.

Left-handed bowler: You drift to the left.

Left- or right-handed bowler: Balance problems during the delivery and at the foul line. Dropping your ball at the foul line. Closing of your shoulders, which means that your shoulders are facing the center of the lane on release.

Late Timing Problems

Right-handed bowler: Ball misses target to the right. Drifting left.

Left-handed bowler: The ball misses its target to the left. Drifting right.

Both left- and right-handed bowler: Your balance is off during the approach and at the foul line. The ball does not come off your hand. Your shoulders are open, which means your shoulders are facing toward the sides of the lane on release.

Drifting

Many bowlers have a comfort zone. Wherever you start at on the approach, you should end up at the foul line on the same board, not at your favorite spot. Some people end up at a different board at the foul line than the one on which they started. For example, they may start at board 10 and end up at board 20. This is called drifting. If you only end up at your favorite spot, you cannot adjust for different shots.

Practice your delivery with no ball in your hand. At the foul line check to see if you finished at the same spot as you started. Do not use your favorite spot. Then repeat it with your bowling ball, releasing it at the foul line. Check to see where you are. You want to end up no more than 2 boards left or right of the board you started on. Alternate your delivery: one time with no ball, another time with the ball. Do this until you can be comfortable wherever you start and finish. Drifting may be why you are missing the target. Get into the habit of checking where you are at the finish of your delivery and comparing it with where you started. Drifting may happen during each step of your delivery. It may happen on only one step of the delivery. You may need a friend to watch you to see how it happens. Do not look at your feet. Timing and the swing of the ball must be checked, because

Bend arm at wrist.

Don't bend at elbow.

they could cause drifting. A high back-swing may cause a right-handed bowler to drift left. A left-handed bowler may drift right for the same reason.

Missing Your Target to the Right

Right-handed bowler: If in your push-away of the ball in your first step, you push the ball to the right and not straight out, in the backswing the ball will go behind your back. This could cause you to drift left. It would also cause the ball to go to the right during your forward swing, missing your target to the right. If your shoulders turn in an open position, toward the right side

of the lane at your release, instead of remaining on your target line, you may miss your target to the right. If you bring your back leg too far to the left at the release, this would turn your shoulders right. It is very, very important to keep your shoulder in your target line at all times.

If your armswing is out, away from your body, you may miss to the right of your target. If your armswing is up to the right at the release, you may miss to the right of your target.

Left-handed bowler: If in your push-away of the ball, in your first step, you push the ball to the right, not straight out, in the backswing the ball will go out, away from your body. This could cause you to drift left. It would also cause the ball to go to the right during your forward swing, missing your target to the right. If your shoulder turns in a closed position toward the middle of the lane, instead of remaining on your target line, you may miss your target to the right. Not releasing the ball early enough in your delivery would cause you to miss to the right of your target.

Missing Your Target to the Left

Right-handed bowler: If your pushaway is to the left, your backswing would go out, away from your body. This could cause you to drift right. Also, in your forward swing, the ball would be going left, missing to the left of your target. If you turn your shoulders left in a closed position instead of remaining on your target line, it would cause you to miss to the left of your target. Not releasing the ball early enough in your delivery would cause you to miss left.

Sometimes you may not trust the decision you make, and think that the ball will not get there. You try to direct the ball by pulling your arm in front of you, especially if it is a hook shot. This causes the ball to miss the target to the left. Always trust the choice you made, even if it turns out that you missed the pin. Your decision-making will get better in time. It is important that you keep your delivery consistent. If you made a good delivery and you miss the pin, you know that you need to adjust your choice. If you did not trust your choice and tried to help it by directing it, you do not know if the choice was bad or the shot was at fault.

Left-handed bowler: If in your push-away of the ball in Step 1, you push the ball to the left, not straight out, in the backswing the ball will go behind your back to the right. This could cause you to drift right. It would also cause the ball to go to the left during your forward swing, missing your target to the left. If your shoulder turns to the open position, toward the left side of the lane, at your release, instead of remaining on your target line, you may miss your target to the left. If you bring your back leg too far to the right at the release, this would turn your shoulders left, causing you to miss left of your target.

If your pushaway isn't straight, it can cause you to drift.

Chapter 9
The Mental Game

After you have learned the physical part of bowling, the mental part becomes the most important. The physical movements will become natural if you let them happen. When you walk from one place to another, you don't think about it. This thinking when we are in the approach is very often what makes us miss. It is all the indecision: Should I do this or maybe do that? Your body will try to do the last thing it thought of before letting go of the ball. Decide what you are going to do before picking up your ball. Then, when you do pick up the ball, position yourself on the approach and go; do not wait.

In bowling, as in other parts of life, our progress sometimes happens in stages. We must not become discouraged. Some things will come easily; others will be harder to learn. There are plateaus in the learning process, and sometimes there's a longer time between growth spurts than at other times. You must have your physical game in control. If your mental part is great and your physical is bad, you may not score well.

When we have confidence in what we are going to do, we are not afraid of doing it. This comes from practicing the basics of bowling, adjusting to lane conditions, and learning how to make spares and splits.

Positive Self-Talk

Each of us has an inner voice that talks to us. This is very often a good thing; it protects us from dangers and tells us right and wrong. In bowling we must teach it to talk to us in only a positive way. We are always ready to say, "Lucky shot!" or "I won't to be able to do that again." We must be honest with our game regarding things that can be improved, but must always look for the good in a shot first.

We are too often ready to beat ourselves up. At a time when my son was not bowling well, he said, "I know I am a good bowler, I am just not bowling well now." This is just the attitude we should have. When you tell yourself not to think of something, what is the first thing on your mind? It is the very thing you told yourself not to think of! Try it yourself; you'll see; this is why it is so important to only think positive. If you are thinking, "Do not pull the ball to the left," you will very likely pull the ball left. Then that person inside of you is ready to say, "See, you cannot bowl."

Instead, think: "Straight up with the arm, make a good followthrough." Most likely it will happen, and if it does not happen yet, it will eventually. We are not perfect. Look at it as a momentary setback and go on. For example, a hitter in baseball who is batting .300 is considered great, and he is only hitting 3 out of 10 times at bat.

I heard a song by Kenny Rogers about a boy who thinks that he is such a good batter that he wants to practice, even if by himself. He tosses the ball up

Keep a positive attitude.

the first time, and swings at it. The ball drops to the ground. He misses it, but he says, "I am the greatest batter." He tosses it up the second time, then swings at it. The ball drops to the ground, and he misses it. He still says, "I am the greatest batter." The third time he tosses it up in the air, he swings at it, and the ball drops to the ground. Now he says, "I am the greatest batter, but I didn't know that I was such a great pitcher."

That is a great attitude — to look at the good, not the bad. It will just put unnecessary pressure on you if you think that every shot has to be "just

right." It will not be just right each time. We are not machines, and even machines break sometimes.

Positive Mental Imagery

Think of mental imagery as a day-dream. It can be of something we have done in the past or something we would like to do. It can become so real that our senses of touch, smell, taste, hearing, and body movements become involved. We are concerned with two types of mental imagery, goal-oriented and process-oriented imagery.

Goal-oriented imagery is also known as outcome-oriented imagery. Goal-oriented imagery is practiced at home, not at the bowling center. At the bowling center it can be counterproductive. Goal-oriented imagery means having images of success. They can be of things you already did or ones you would like to do — for example, bowling consecutive strikes to win a game; bowling what is needed in the 10th frame to win the game; making all your spares in a game.

Process-oriented imagery focuses on the process of bowling itself. Picture yourself relaxed, getting ready to bowl. See yourself in a perfect stance, going into a perfect delivery, releasing the ball perfectly. The ball will worry about knocking down the pins, not you. If you are relaxed and deliver the ball well, you will get good results — no need to worry.

Every time you get up to bowl, it is just you and the pins. Every time you

better at it, you will be able to do it in a crowd. If you have ever watched Mark McGwire in the batter's box, you may recall that every time he gets ready to bat, he stands there with his eyes closed. It seems that he is doing mental imagery in preparation for batting. He did not get a hit every time at bat, but he did break a single-season home-run hitting record.

Relaxation and Breathing

As well as practicing imagery, it's important to practice relaxation and breathing techniques, which will help you release anxiety and stress before you begin to bowl, as well as during a game. They should be practiced alone in a quiet place, several times a week. The more you practice, the better you become. Soothing music will help reduce outside distractions. Breathe from the diaphragm. The stomach should rise and fall, not the chest. Breathe in through the nose and out through the mouth, deeply and slowly. Do not hold your breath or force your breath out. As you are breathing in, bring all your anxiety and stress to your diaphragm. Now release it as you are breathing out. Enjoy the feeling of becoming relaxed, with all the stress leaving your body. With every breath, you should become more relaxed.

throw the ball, it has to be the best you can do. There is never a time you have to worry. Every time is equal to the next. Imagery needs to be practiced. The more you practice, the easier it will become. Why does practicing imagery work in helping you become a better bowler? When you imagine yourself bowling, you are programming your subconscious mind to do the series of movements you are imaging. You put the instruction in place, step on the approach, and go. Do not think any more at this point. By practicing imagery, these movements will became natural. Practice imagery in a quiet place alone at first; as you become

Progressive Muscle Relaxation

It's important to be able to repeat your delivery in a fluid manner with a relaxed armswing. You need to be relaxed. Many times we believe that we are relaxed when we are not. It may be that some muscles are tight all the time, or during a stressful moment, or for certain shots. Not being relaxed could cause you to miss your shot. With the help of these techniques, you will become aware of times when you are not relaxed.

As with imagery, relaxation, and breathing, progressive muscle relaxation is best practiced alone in a quiet place. Start with your shoulders. Tighten the muscles in your right shoulder, and concentrate on how this feels. Now relax that shoulder, concentrate on how this feels, and you will feel the tension leave your body. Next, do the left shoulder, and then do both shoulders, each time concentrating on how that part feels. Your muscles will tighten, then become loose, and you will feel the tension leave your body. Next do the muscles in your upper arms, then the lower arms, the fingers, back, stomach, legs, feet, even your head, eyes, and tongue. You want to become familiar with how your muscles feel when tight and loose. Then, during a game, or even in your everyday life, you will be able to feel tension and release it with the use of mental imagery, relaxation, breathing, and muscle relaxation techniques.

Glossary

Alley: (1) an individual lane; (2) the entire bowling place.

Angle of entry: Angle, measured in comparison to the boards, at which the bowling ball hits the 1-3 pocket (1-2 pocket for lefties) after completing its path down the lane.

Approach: The area on which a bowler steps in delivering the ball.

Arc: A ball path from the foul line to the head pin that does not have a sharply defined breakpoint.

Axis of rotation: Imaginary line, perpendicular to the ball track, around which a bowling ball rotates during its path down the lane.

Axis point: One of the two endpoints of the axis of rotation.

Axis tilt: Angle between axis of rotation and a horizontal plane through the middle of the ball. The angle is created by the bowler at the release of the ball by the angle of his fingers to the swing.

Back end: The 20 feet of the lane right before the head (#1) pin.

Back of hole: Portion of hole facing away from the center of the grip.

Backswing: Portion of bowler's swing from the time the ball passes the side of the body until the ball reaches the highest point of the swing behind him.

Backup ball: Ball that veers from the bowler's inside to the outside on the lane. Also called a reverse hook.

Balance arm: Nonbowling arm.

Ball reaction: Change in direction of the ball's path.

Ball track: Area of the bowling ball that makes contact with the lane's surface during its path down the lane. Because of revolving motion, this area is usually in the form of a ring or rings around the ball.

Bevel: Rounded edge of a hole drilled in a bowling ball.

Boards: The lane is made up of 39 individual strips of wood called boards, running down the lane, pieced together to comprise the surface.

Bowling pins. Tall, curved wooden objects, covered in plastic, which are knocked down to gain points.

Breakpoint: In the trajectory (path) of a bowling ball, the point at which the ball makes its greatest change in direction.

Bridge: Distance between the finger holes on the bowling ball.

Carrydown: Moving of oil lane conditioner down the lane, caused by the passage of bowling balls over it.

Channels. *See* Gutters.

Coefficient of friction: An indicator of the surface character of an object (for example, a bowling ball). Different surfaces have different coefficients of friction. Surfaces with a higher coefficient of friction are harder to slide on than ones with a lower coefficient of friction.

Conditioner: Oil that is put on the lane to protect it. The amount of conditioner and its location affect the way the ball rolls.

Conventional grip: Grip in which the bowler places his/her two fingers into the ball up to the second knuckle joints.

The fingers are bent at a 90° angle at the second joint.

Coverstock: The material that makes up the outer shell of the ball. Coverstocks are described as "aggressive" (high friction, tends to hook on dry boards), "medium" (less tendency to hook), or "mellow" (having the lowest friction).

Cranker: Bowler who generates revolutions by a cupped wrist, bent elbow, or muscled armswing, rather than accuracy, to succeed.

Deflection: Amount of turning away from its previous path that a bowling ball makes, after making contact with any pin.

Delivery: The steps and swing of the ball that the bowler makes, which end in releasing the ball to roll down the lane.

Dull finish: Unpolished surface of a bowling ball. In general, a dull bowling ball is one in which the pores are open and clean.

Dynamics: Characteristics of the mass of a bowling ball that affect the way it moves.

Error: A missed spare.

Fingertip grip: Style of grip in which the bowler inserts fingers into the ball up to the first joint, while placing the entire thumb in the ball.

Followthrough: Portion of bowler's delivery that occurs after the release of the ball.

Forward pitch: The drilled hole, either finger or thumb, is angled toward the center line of the grip.

Foul: A foul occurs when part of the player's body encroaches on or goes beyond the foul line and touches any part of the lane, equipment, or building during or after releasing the ball.

Foul line: The line that separates the approach from the beginning of the playing surface of the lane.

Frame: One-tenth of a game.

Friction: The force that resists the motion of one surface in relation to another surface with which it is in contact. Surfaces, even smooth ones, resist motion, but rough surfaces resist more than smooth ones.

Front of hole: Portion of the hole facing toward the center of the bowler's grip.

Full roller: A ball whose track passes between the thumb hole and finger holes; the track equals the circumference of the ball in a full roller.

Gripper/squeezer: Someone who holds on to the ball with excessive force.

Gutter ball: Delivery that rolls off the lane into the gutter.

Gutters: Channels to the right and left of the playing surface that catch balls that roll off the lane.

Head pin: The #1 pin.

Heads: Portion of the lane from the foul line to the arrow markings, which are generally located 15 to 18 feet down the lane.

Heavy hit: A pocket shot that makes more contact with the head pin than an ideal shot should.

High-performance balls: Balls designed to create specific reactions for different bowlers.

High track: A track on the bowling ball outside of the thumb hole and finger holes that is no more than an inch from either.

Hitting the ball: Very fast acceleration of the hand around the ball, from under the ball to the side at the release point.

Hook: Amount, measured in boards and angle, that a bowling ball turns from its original path in its trip down the lane.

Hook angle: Angle at which the bowling ball changes direction at its breakpoint.

Hook ball: Ball that follows a bent path to the pins from the bowler's outside (swingside) to the inside.

Hook potential: Degree to which the properties designed into a bowling ball aid in its potential for moving over boards during its path down the lane.

IBPSIA: International Bowling Pro Shop & Instructors Association Inc.

Inside: The portion of the lane bounded by ten boards on each side: the central 19 boards.

Line: Intended path of the ball down the lane.

Loft: Distance the ball travels after it is released before it makes contact with the lane surface.

Lofting: Throwing the ball in the air beyond the foul line.

Low track: A track on the bowling ball outside the finger holes and thumb hole, but more than two inches from either.

Make: (v.) To knock down all pins that are standing.

Mark: Point on the lane at which the bowler is aiming.

Miss: An error, a missed spare.

Pin (regarding a ball): A small round discoloration on a bowling ball that marks the top of the weight block.

Pin action: The manner in which the pins react to the impact of the bowling ball.

Pin carry: The ability of a ball to knock down pins.

Pinfall: The number of pins knocked down by a ball.

Pitch: The angle at which a hole is drilled into a bowling ball compared to the geometric center (axis) of the ball. Reverse pitch is drilling that heads away from the center of the ball. Forward pitch is towards the center of the ball.

Pocket: Area between the #1 and #2 pins for a left-handed bowler and between the #1 and #3 pins for a right-handed bowler.

Positive axis point (PAP): The point on the surface of the ball that is the end of the ball's axis of rotation, on the positive side of the ball (the same side as the little finger).

Preferred spin axis (PSA): The axis about which the bowling ball wants to rotate.

Pulling the ball: Result when the bowler misses his/her target to the inside of the armswing's intended direction.

Pushaway: Portion of delivery in which the bowler sets the ball in motion.

Rack: A formation of pins.

Radius of gyration (RG): Distance from middle of the bowling ball at which the mass (weight) effectively is located. The RG affects how fast a ball begins to rotate.

Release: Point in the delivery at which the ball leaves the hand.

Revolutions: The number of times the bowling ball makes a complete rotation about its axis during its path down the lane, before it reaches the pins. The higher the number, the more hitting power usually results.

Rotation: Movement of any mass that moves around an axis, for example, the earth.

Rotational energy: Spin or revolutions of the ball, given by the bowler at the moment of release.

Shell: The outer portion of a bowling ball, surrounding the core.

Shiny ball: A ball that looks glossy. In general, shiny balls have fewer open/exposed pores than dull balls.

Skid: The portion of the bowling ball's path in which the ball is actually not rolling but is instead sliding down the lane.

Snap: A ball path that has a sharp, defined breakpoint.

Span: Distance from the edge of the thumb hole nearest to the ball's center to the edge of a finger hole that is nearest to the center.

Spare: (n.) The second ball's knocking down all pins that were left standing after the first-ball attempt of the frame. Symbol is a slash / on the scoresheet.

Split: Pins left standing with pins missing in between them after the first ball of a frame has been thrown. The symbol for a split is an open circle or the symbol S.

Stance: The way the bowler stands in the starting position.

Strike: (n.) Knocking down all 10 pins with the first ball thrown in a frame is called a strike. Symbol: X.

Stroker: Someone who has smooth swing and delivery without sudden acceleration.

Surface: The texture, both finish and hardness, of a bowling ball.

Swingside: The side of your body on which you are swinging the ball.

System of bowling: ABC/WIBC regulations concerning balls, pins, lanes, and dressing distribution.

Target point: Location at which you aim, such as an arrow marked on the lane.

Track flare: Refers to the migration of the bowling ball's track as a result of the changes in its axis of rotation from the axis it had when it was released to final axis it has when it hits the pins during its path down the lane. A new ball surface touches the lane on each revolution when the ball has large flare, which is good for oily lane conditions. The result can be seen as several distinct oil rings around the ball. Balls are rated as to flare potential, the maximum amount the axis of the ball can migrate, given the construction of the ball.

USA Bowling Assn.: The official national governing body of amateur bowling in the United States. It funds and oversees Team USA, the official bowling team representing the United States. This organization also develops and conducts coaching certification programs as well as bowling clinics for beginning, intermediate, and advanced bowlers.

Weight block: A dense piece of material found in the interior of a bowling ball.

Weight hole: A nongripping hole that is used to achieve a specific legal imbalance in a bowling ball; the hole cannot be more than 1¼ inches in diameter.

Index